**PERSONAL LEADERSHIP**

# Personal Leadership

A Practical Approach
for Achieving Individual and
Organizational Freedom

**RICHARD W. JAMES**

CRISP PUBLICATIONS

MENLO PARK, CALIFORNIA

MANAGING EDITOR: George Young

EDITOR: Sal Glynn

COVER DESIGN & PRODUCTION: Fifth Street Design

PAGE DESIGN & TYPESETTING: Colored Horse Studios
This book has been typeset in Trump Mediaeval and Bailey Sans

PRINTER: Von Hoffmann Graphics, Inc.

Copyright © 2001 Crisp Publications, Inc.

All rights reserved. No part of this book may be reproduced or transmitted in any form or by any means now known or to be invented, electronic or mechanical, including photocopying, recording, or by any information storage or retrieval system without written permission from the author or publisher, except for the brief inclusion of quotation in a review. Printed in the United States of America.

Library of Congress Card Catalog Number: 00-111321
ISBN 1-56052-591-6

01 02 03 04   10 9 8 7 6 5 4 3 2 1

## Dedication

To each and every one of us on this planet.
We are all heroes and heroines that are consciously
and unconsciously working together
to pave the way
for successful living
in the new millennium.

**ACKNOWLEDGMENTS**

Doug Krug and Ed Oakley are co-authors of the book *Enlightened Leadership: Getting to the Heart of Change* (New York: Simon and Schuster, 1999). The mission of their company and the message of the book is as follows:

> "We believe that the renewal of any organization is based on the personal and professional fulfillment of its people.
> "Our mission is to facilitate a process of self-discovery in people that awakens the leader within them, unlocks their creativity, ignites their spirit of cooperation, and sets them on a never-ending quest for continuous improvement.
> "It is the power and reward of Enlightened Leadership to align the hearts, the spirits, and the dreams of people in order to create organizations in which there is joy in the work and satisfaction in the accomplishment."

Many thanks to Enlightened Leadership International and Simon and Schuster for giving their permission to share some of the principles they teach.

## ABOUT THE AUTHOR

Richard W. James is an entrepreneur, developing growth companies in many various industries. His business career began as a CPA with one of the largest accounting firms in the world. He left public accounting to experience private enterprise with a large regional restaurant/motel chain. It was with this organization that Mr. James began discovering that his real passion in life was people, not numbers.

He became CFO and later president of a large financial planning firm. It was in these capacities that he became fascinated with management and leadership. Along with his executive team, he participated in Stephen R. Covey's year-long Executive Excellence course, taught by Dr. Covey. This experience began expanding his passion to experience all that is possible in all aspects of life for himself and others, while creating a model of the successful twenty-first century leader and organization that achieves unprecedented results through people.

He purchased a training company and helped take it from $400,000 annual sales to over $10,000,000 in three years. Later he became part of a coaching company, assisting individuals in realizing their full potential. He then helped expand another training company, which eventually led him to join the team at Enlightened Leadership International where he served as general manager and president. Some of the principles and tools presented in this book have come from this experience.

Currently Mr. James is enjoying his highest passion, developing "leadership ranches" all over the world in which fun-filled, open, and supportive environments are created for deeper, quicker learning and application of life changing Principles, Attitudes and Practices—a physical "heaven on earth," dedicated to assisting people in bringing forth the best that is within them and help to create what they want in their lives.

Mr. James life's mission is to:
    Experience the excitement of realizing his full potential as to
        Who he can be
        What he can accomplish

And all that he chooses to have in life
While serving others in accomplishing the same!

Assist organizations in uniting the minds, bodies, and hearts of their people in achieving all the desired results they choose to accomplish.

Create physical environments for assisting people in
- Healing
- Personal development
- Creating and achieving desired results.

If you are interested in joining and networking with others in accomplishing all that is possible, while assisting others and organizations in doing the same, call (866) YOU-LEAD.

## Table of Contents

Preface ..................................................................... xii

Chapter One: Getting Results ................................................. 1
    What the World Needs Now ............................................... 2
    Global Vision and Core Belief .......................................... 3
    Freedom Through Personal Responsibility ................................ 5
    The New Millennium ..................................................... 7
    Three Stages of Growth—Present and Future .............................. 9
    Important Foundation Beliefs .......................................... 10
    Personal Leadership: A Practical Approach for Achieving Individual and Organizational Freedom ....... 10
    Basic Beliefs ......................................................... 12
    The Call .............................................................. 13
    Today, By Choice, I Am... ............................................. 14

Chapter Two: Increasing Your Freedom for Getting More Results ............... 17
    How Life Works ........................................................ 17
    Today, By Choice, I Am... ............................................. 24

Chapter Three: A Simple Plan for Managing Change and Accomplishing More .... 25
    Today, By Choice, I Am... ............................................. 31

Chapter Four: Five Key Concepts for Enhancing Personal Leadership .......... 32
    Knowledge Plus Experience ............................................. 32
    Power Pausing ......................................................... 37
    Spend Time with Truth ................................................. 38
    Stewardship and Accountability ........................................ 39
    Sharing Experiences ................................................... 41
    Today, By Choice, I Am... ............................................. 43

Chapter Five: The Power of Being Principle-Centered, Attitude-Driven,
and Practice-Committed............................................ 44
    The Link Between Principles, Attitudes, and Practices............. 44
    Mind, Body, and the Divine....................................... 44
    The Capacity of the Human Mind................................... 48
    Feelings and Emotions in Personal Leadership...................... 52
    Keys to Learning Through the Mind and Body....................... 54
    The Divine....................................................... 57
    Today, By Choice, I Am........................................... 68

Chapter Six: Individual and Organizational Freedom..................... 69
    Principle: Choice................................................ 69
    Attitude: Self-Responsibility.................................... 71
    Attitude: Courage................................................ 73
    Practice: Practicing, Practicing, Every Day...................... 74
    Practice: Results Driven......................................... 75
    Practice: Living from Passion.................................... 76
    Today, By Choice, I Am........................................... 79

Chapter Seven: The Power of One........................................ 80
    Who are We?...................................................... 80
    Freedom Through "Resetting the Zero"............................. 81
    Principle: Belief in Who We Are.................................. 87
    Attitude: All Things are Possible................................ 89
    Practice: Being Aware............................................ 90
    Practice: Leading from Within.................................... 91
    Practice: Acting as If........................................... 95
    Shared Leadership................................................ 95
    Teams Working Effectively Together............................... 97
    Today, By Choice, I Am........................................... 99

Chapter Eight: Freedom to Thrive on Change............................ 100
    Maintaining versus Creating..................................... 101
    Management versus Leadership.................................... 102
    Change Without Resistance....................................... 103
    Principle: Continuous Renewal/Change............................ 105
    Attitude: The "Blessing" of Opposition.......................... 106

Practice: Running on Freedom Questions . . . . . . . . . . . . . . . . . . . . . . 107
Practice: The Infinite Freedom and Power of Questions . . . . . . . . . . . . . 107
Practice: Personal Leadership Guidelines . . . . . . . . . . . . . . . . . . . . . 112
Practice: Listening with the Heart. . . . . . . . . . . . . . . . . . . . . . . . . 116
What it Takes to Make a Major Change . . . . . . . . . . . . . . . . . . . . . 117
Today, By Choice, I Am... . . . . . . . . . . . . . . . . . . . . . . . . . . . . 119

Chapter Nine: The Key to Freedom . . . . . . . . . . . . . . . . . . . . . . . . . . 120
Principle: Integrity. . . . . . . . . . . . . . . . . . . . . . . . . . . . . . . . . 120
Attitude: Obedience. . . . . . . . . . . . . . . . . . . . . . . . . . . . . . . . 121
Practice: Making and Keeping Commitments . . . . . . . . . . . . . . . . . . 122
Today, By Choice, I Am... . . . . . . . . . . . . . . . . . . . . . . . . . . . . 125

Chapter Ten: "Staying on a Roll"—Keeping the Momentum Going. . . . . . . . . 126
Principle: Balance. . . . . . . . . . . . . . . . . . . . . . . . . . . . . . . . . 126
Attitude: Positive Focus. . . . . . . . . . . . . . . . . . . . . . . . . . . . . . 130
Attitude: Play. . . . . . . . . . . . . . . . . . . . . . . . . . . . . . . . . . . 132
Practice: The Four C's for Sustainable Growth . . . . . . . . . . . . . . . . . 133
Practice: The Power of Symbols. . . . . . . . . . . . . . . . . . . . . . . . . 135
Today, By Choice, I Am... . . . . . . . . . . . . . . . . . . . . . . . . . . . . 139

Chapter Eleven: Freedom for Experiencing All and More of Desired Results . . . 140
Principle: Law of the Harvest . . . . . . . . . . . . . . . . . . . . . . . . . . 140
Attitude: Gratitude . . . . . . . . . . . . . . . . . . . . . . . . . . . . . . . . 142
Practice: Service to People and Organizations . . . . . . . . . . . . . . . . . 143
Today, By Choice, I Am... . . . . . . . . . . . . . . . . . . . . . . . . . . . . 145

Chapter Twelve: Freedom in Realizing Your Full Potential . . . . . . . . . . . . . 146
Love versus Fear. . . . . . . . . . . . . . . . . . . . . . . . . . . . . . . . . . 147
The Fruits of Deep and Sincere Caring . . . . . . . . . . . . . . . . . . . . . 149
Personal Leadership in Relationships . . . . . . . . . . . . . . . . . . . . . . 149
Freedom Cycle for Achieving Results . . . . . . . . . . . . . . . . . . . . . . 153
What is Really Possible to Achieve as Individuals and Organizations? . . . 155
Today, By Choice, I Am... . . . . . . . . . . . . . . . . . . . . . . . . . . . . 157

Afterword. . . . . . . . . . . . . . . . . . . . . . . . . . . . . . . . . . . . . . . . 158

Appendices

- Appendix A: Concepts and Definitions . . . . . . . . . . . . . . . . . . . . . . . . . . 160
- Appendix B: Freedom Through Personal Leadership . . . . . . . . . . . . . . . . . 162
- Appendix C: Things That Affect the Flow for Desired Results . . . . . . . . . . 163
- Appendix D: Change Master Plan. . . . . . . . . . . . . . . . . . . . . . . . . . . . . . 164
- Appendix E: How We are Evolving in the New Millennium . . . . . . . . . . . 166
- Appendix F: Twelve Habits for Leading from Within (Intuition) . . . . . . . . . 167
- Appendix G: Differences in Directing Your Life from the Mind (Logic) versus the Divine. . . . . . . . . . . . . . . . . . . . . . . 170
- Appendix H: Personal Leadership Questions . . . . . . . . . . . . . . . . . . . . . . 171
- Appendix I: Completing the Past Year . . . . . . . . . . . . . . . . . . . . . . . . . . 178
- Appendix J: Twelve Areas of Balance . . . . . . . . . . . . . . . . . . . . . . . . . . . 180
- Appendix K: Preparing Your Personal Life Plan . . . . . . . . . . . . . . . . . . . . 181
- Appendix L: Vision for Organizations. . . . . . . . . . . . . . . . . . . . . . . . . . . 183
- Appendix M: Sixty Signs You are Increasing Your Power to Love and Honor 185
- Appendix N: Freedom Questions . . . . . . . . . . . . . . . . . . . . . . . . . . . . . . 188
- Appendix O: Signs of Being a Victim . . . . . . . . . . . . . . . . . . . . . . . . . . . 191
- Appendix P: High Priority Reading List . . . . . . . . . . . . . . . . . . . . . . . . . 192

## PREFACE

What will be different in your life as a result of this book?

The answer to this question is: *It's all up to you!* This is not about dumping new information into your mind that will suddenly have an impact in your personal and business life. People who have consistently taken off the "roller skates of life" and applied these simple attitudes and principles have had immediate results in their personal and business lives. This book can apply effectively to your private life as well. The impact on your life, and how quickly it affects your daily success, depends on taking time to thoroughly understand and apply the concepts shared in these pages.

The intent of this book is not to tell you the right way, or best way of doing things, or how you should think or behave. It is about sharing the experiences I have had personally and those I have observed, with the hope that it will open up ways for you to get the truths and guidance for your life, getting the very best from yourself, and the results you desire. *Personal Leadership* will open you up to the new potential and limitless possibilities you and the organizations you are part of can achieve.

A few clients have felt this is old stuff they have heard before. They may know it, but they do not apply it. Test these principles, focus on implementing them, and the results will be astonishing. Tens of thousands of people have successfully used this information. And it is long lasting.

Truth comes in various forms, and from various sources. Truth will come from all of life if we "stay awake" and look! Quotes used throughout *Personal Leadership* come from a wide range of leaders. The main content is kept as simple as possible, with the Appendices giving more detailed information. What is presented in the entire book is not inclusive of the whole truth that is available, it is only a beginning. It is up to you to add your truth.

**Note:** Repetition breeds learning. Certain words and concepts in *Personal Leadership* are purposely repeated throughout the book in order to bring greater impact in the learning process. See Appendix A on page 160 for special definitions that apply to certain words used in this book.

# 1
## GETTING RESULTS

*Personal Leadership* is about getting results. More importantly, it's about getting those results more smoothly, easily, faster, and even more abundantly than ever before. This is the author's definition of *True Freedom*.

This book is also about assisting all who desire, *to make a choice*, about being a *mentor* to others, and a *model* in all organizations they serve, in getting more of the results they desire.

This book suggests that all of this is accomplished by focusing more attention on *who we are,* versus working harder and harder.

This book gives evidence and testimony that in order to experience results that are not only what we think we want, but *all that is possible*, we must *"Be":*

Principle-centered

Attitude-driven

and Practice-committed!

These six words, categorized into three areas, are carefully selected as the essence of the "How To" accomplish True Freedom, as defined above.

The "How To" is simply answered by involving our whole being in the process of getting results. The Divine (see Appendix A) within us is hopefully the Source for our selection of which principles we choose to guide our life. Then the challenge becomes getting our whole being to act and speak from those values and principles. This is where the practices come in, making it possible for the body to have the power to live by the principles selected. And the mind is the link between the two, the bridge that makes possible achieving our desired results and more. This is where the attitudes play a significant role. The principles, attitudes, and practices are all needed. Attention needs to be given by each of us to our whole being (the Divine, mind, and body) in this process of achieving all that is possible.

What if you have never focused much on who you are and not sure if you have the passion to improve, change, and grow? If there is the slightest willingness to get more of the results you want in life, and you have some degree of trust that who you are is a key to getting those results, then let this willingness and trust begin working inside you, and you will be amazed at how these desires will grow, until you become passionate about this whole process of growth and achievement—a true hero or heroine of the new millennium!

A true story comes from Jerry Schemmel's miraculous survival from the United Airlines crash in Sioux City, Iowa in 1989. After he escaped the burning wreckage of the plane, he heard a baby's cry and went back into the smoke and flames of the burning fuselage to rescue an 11-month-old baby girl who had become separated from her parents. Many in the press said he was a hero. He claimed that what he did was instinctive, and without premeditation. However, as he reflected on the incident in the months afterwards, he came to some interesting conclusions:

> The purest form of heroism does not involve a single act.
> A hero is one who, over an extended period of time, is a person of strength and integrity in the face of adversity that is part of everyday life.
> Heroism is measured by how someone lives his/her life, by his/her everyday attitudes and actions.

Therefore, since all who are on Earth are heroes and heroines, each of us needs to be everything that we can be, in order to do more good in the world through the things we accomplish individually, with others, and with the organizations (see Appendix A) we are part of.

Out of the small words and actions of our lives, from day to day, great things are accomplished. This is also the message of this book.

This book is about making a significant impact (not an impression!) in our lives, in others, and the organizations we have chosen to be part of.

## What the World Needs Now

People! Each one of us is the most important source for significantly and practically moving the world forward with unprecedented success. Each of us, in relationship with ourselves and each other, are the most important key to realizing achievements that we have only dreamed about. The world needs organizations who choose to have, as their highest ideal, a commitment to consistently focus resources on developing the full potential of their people, individually and collectively, creating models of the greatest success possible. The "Global Vision and Core Belief" that follows is created as a suggested unifying desired result for each of us to align with and to be passionate about, in our own unique ways.

# Global Vision and Core Belief

## GLOBAL VISION: THE ESSENCE OF PERSONAL LEADERSHIP

To obtain the *greatest desired results possible*
in the new millennium,
as individuals and as organizations
the world needs more
*People*
who *proactively* and *passionately*
bring forth more of the very best that is within them,
in *service* to other *people* and *organizations*,
in generating results for the highest good of all.
And
*Organizations*
who *balance* their needs
for desired *bottom line results*
with sincere *caring*,
*honoring*,
and *development* of all individuals
that make up their organization,
while focusing on learning to work together in harmony.
And the circumstances, events, and conditions in the new
millennium, throughout the world,
within each organization,
will *continue* to get our attention
in order to move us further in these directions.

When any organization (see Appendix A) dedicates itself to its people, and honors them for being of great value, whatever their title or function, unlimited results occur. The honoring must go beyond words in a mission statement, a slogan on a truck ("our people make the difference"), or anywhere else for the world to read. "Walking the talk," (what is professed directly affects daily thoughts, feelings, words, and actions) must be an organization's number one priority!

This book is about increasing true freedom within individuals and organizations for achieving more and greater desired results than ever before, and sustaining results over time without cyclical ups and downs.

Each person bringing forth her/his best—and each organization doing its best to be caring and honoring with each and every team member—will have a significant impact on bringing this level of achievement about.

CHAPTER ONE: GETTING RESULTS

## CORNERSTONE BELIEF

> "You cannot teach a man anything. You can only help him discover it within himself." —GALILEO GALILEI

The cornerstone belief of this book is simple: the solutions for a person's life are within that person. Similarly, the solutions for an organization's success are within the people that make up the organization. The concepts, Principles, Attitudes, and Practices that are shared in this book will assist you in consistently getting to those solutions, thus gaining more true freedom to achieve greater results.

Most people, and most organizations, do not need more new information. What is needed is to bring more of the best that is within each of us, and more of the best within the organizations we are part of, to realize greater results. The Principles, Attitudes, and Practices shared in this book are fundamental ones that create a significant impact on people's and organization's success throughout the world every day.

This simple illustration shows the essence of the core belief in an image easy to remember. The oil rig symbolizes the mind and body (or the organization). The oil at the bottom symbolizes the available answers and solutions for ourselves and the organizations we are part of.

The figure on the *left* symbolizes our current abilities, however small or great, to tap into those answers and solutions. The figure on the *right* shows the significant difference in your life for getting more of the results you seek. By applying these concepts, the amount of "oil" we get access to is in direct proportion to the application of these Principles, Attitudes, and Practices.

Our freedom to tap into this reservoir of "oil" that we carry within ourselves is one of the key purposes of life—the highest level of results we achieve in life are directly related to our belief in the ability to get to these resources. These resources are infinite in supply, and are not based on some special God-given gift, talent, or ordination.

> "If you want to be prosperous for a year, grow grain.
> If you want to be prosperous for ten years grow trees.
> If you want to be prosperous for a lifetime, grow people." —PROVERB

## Freedom through Personal Responsibility

For most people, freedom is a choice, not something that is given. Organizations are counseled to empower their people for the greatest success. But in an organizational environment, true empowerment is a choice by each person, after the organization has given them the power to act. Choosing to be empowered, and how to bring forth your best at all times, is the essence of *Personal Leadership*.

Historically, a "few" have shown great power in achieving results through what they were able to "do." But in the new millennium, many more powerful leaders need to come forth, if not the majority of us, in reaching to "be" better—a personal continuous change process! Greater power to achieve more desired results comes as more and more people balance "being" with "doing" in each organization.

What is suggested here is that as we become truly the best we can be (individually and as organizations), real freedom to achieve greater, and more abundant desired results, will occur more smoothly and with less effort. Stated another way, the old adage, "If you want something in your life, you have to work hard at it," is outdated. This is an old world paradigm that is proving to be inadequate in the new millennium to accomplish unprecedented results.

Many people have been significantly victimized, abused, or hurt in some way, and live from the "I am a victim" mindset. The truth is that we all have a choice about how we respond to life, and how much we take responsibility in what we create for our lives and for our organizations.

*Personal Leadership* is about you, for it is up to you to get the *results* you choose to have in your life, and the goals/results each organization you are a part of. It is about your desire to create the ability to achieve; and to accomplish those results easier and quicker!

We are all leaders, *now!* This is not about *becoming* a leader, which gives the connotation that we are not leaders now, or that somehow we have things that are wrong with us, or bad, and that needs "fixing." Accepting ourselves for who we are right now, and applying truth that consistently increases our leadership qualities, is vital to increasing our freedom (see Appendix A).

### BELIEFS, VALUES, HABITS, ATTITUDES

Creating more freedom for getting the results you want may take eliminating some of the old beliefs, values, habits, attitudes, behaviors, thought patterns, and words spoken that no longer serve you in getting what you want. We sometimes have a very difficult time letting go of certain patterns that have been established for years, even when they cause us pain! For example, continuing to eat too much leads to more weight than is good for us; or a company that is so comfortable with what and how they do business, they never take time to look at new things.

As pointed out earlier, most individuals and organizations run their lives on the belief that... "if it's worthwhile, you must work long and hard to get it."

Is this your personal belief? ___ Yes ___ No

Is this a belief and an expectation of you within the organizations you work for? ___ Yes ___ No

If your answer is yes, how willing and open are you and your organization to believe you can get results quicker, easier, and more abundantly than ever before?

_____
_____
_____
_____

How easy will it be to let go of the *habit* of hard work to get what you want? And all the stress and pressure you were under to accomplish what you desired?

_____
_____
_____
_____

If in this example you had the "work hard" belief, and had a difficult time thinking of letting it go, then the quantity and quality of change in your life to get more desired results may prove much more difficult. Having the ability to let go of old beliefs and habits, and create new paradigms for yourself will be a powerful influence in your life, and with the organizations you are a part of.

When we bring forth more of the best we can "be," we are able to tap into that infinite reserve of "oil" that brings us answers and solutions about how to get the results we want. Some call this our intuition. Regardless of what name we put to it, we do less "doing" (hard work), and the results we choose to have in our life become smoother, easier, and require less effort. We discover how to not waste time and energy on things that have no real value for generating our results.

## The New Millennium

"Experts" have said that in the new millennium we will have a choice to bring forth the best that is within us, or we will be forced to adapt because of the dramatic changes that are taking place so quickly. Although they use different words, the experts have the same message about the new millennium: the amount of change, and the speed at which it will come, will all increase. Here is a summary of the expert's thoughts:
- Change is the only constant in our life today.
- The rapid pace of change makes obsolete our businesses, our jobs, and our investment strategies.
- Sweeping economic and social changes are coming.
- Catastrophic changes in all areas of life are just ahead of us.
- Change will only accelerate dramatically in the coming decades.

"… (the new millennium is) a time of sweeping change that threatens old ways of thinking and doing business."
—HENRY S. DENT, JR.,
*The Roaring 2000s*

Things are changing so rapidly that we don't have time to become comfortable with a certain way of doing things. We are forced to adapt quickly to everything changing around us. Just look at the drastic changes that occurred in the educational climate from the first half of the twentieth century to the second half. Today schools are facing unthinkable new threats: violence and mass murder, a long way from unfinished homework.

**TOP TEN SCHOOL PROBLEMS**

| ▶ 1900–1950 | ▶ 1950–2000 |
|---|---|
| 1. Truancy | 1. Violence |
| 2. Running in the halls | 2. Stealing |
| 3. Talking in class | 3. Forcible rape |
| 4. Incomplete homework | 4. Teacher abuse |
| 5. Loitering | 5. Carrying weapons |
| 6. Books not returned | 6. Vandalism |
| 7. Gum in class | 7. Substance abuse |
| 8. Talking in study hall | 8. Arson |
| 9. Broken windows | 9. Rebellion against authority |
| 10. Graffiti | 10. Gang warfare |

Excerpted from *The Battle for the Family* by Tim LaHaye.

A few experts also refer to a *third* choice amid these dramatic changes: some may choose to "check out" because of all the chaos, turmoil, and uncontrolled and uncertain conditions in our fast-paced world. But there is a fourth way—we can to choose to *thrive on change,* not just survive or check out!

CHAPTER ONE: GETTING RESULTS

There is a growing shift from the traditional idea of a leader appearing and she or he leading us toward achieving desired results, to a new kind of leadership needing to be drawn from each of us. We *all* need to look to ourselves in contributing more to the success in our own world, in the lives of the organizations we are part of, and in the overall progress of the entire planet.

Read and carefully ponder these two quotes by successful business leaders:

The Trillion Dollar Vision of Dee Ward Hock
(retired leader in the banking industry)
"We are at that very point in time when a 400-year-old age is dying and another is struggling to be born—a shifting of culture, science, society, and institutions enormously greater than the world has ever experienced. Ahead, the possibility of the regeneration of individuality, liberty, community, and ethics such as the world has never known, and a harmony with nature, with one another, and with the divine intelligence such as the world has never dreamed."

*The Roaring 2000s*—Harry S. Dent. Jr.
"Surveys of happiness in this country (America) have shown that wealth affects the sense of well-being by a factor of only two percent. Happiness is more about relationship, friends, family, and community ... and a balanced life. It's more fundamentally about living, learning, experiencing, and growing as a human being. It's ultimately about evolution (change). It's what you do with your life that counts...."

The essence of successful living in the years ahead requires each of us to take responsibility for choosing the principles, attitudes, and practices that will assist in bringing out the very best within ourselves, then we can unite with others of like minds and hearts in helping any organization we are part of to achieve their desired goals/results. In this way we become capable of thriving on change, not just surviving, and our true freedom to excel dramatically increases.

The new millennium will be totally different than what we have seen and experienced in the past. To move into the present and future will mean letting go of some, or all, of the past. It just will not look and feel the same.

Successful twenty-first century leadership will require:
- As many people as possible within an organization contributing their very best, not just depending on one leader to tell people the "right" way.

- A focus on honoring everyone within the organization.
- A focus on integrating personal life with business life so they both thrive.
- Greater team, community, and family environments where people are working together, growing together, all for a common goal/vision.

The gap between what one says and what one does needs to grow smaller and smaller. This is also true for any organization. "Walking the talk" (the integrity of the people and the organization) is vital to getting desired results more quickly and more easily.

Each one of us, in our own way, for our own specific purposes in life, will need to be *change masters* (having the ability to go with the flow and adapt to rapidly changing conditions, relationships, and environment).

Our "inner world" (who we are) will need to become more aligned with our "outer world" (what we are doing and saying and who is involved with what we do and say) in order to maintain peace and happiness.

## Three Stages of Growth—Present and Future

### A FRESH LOOK INTO OUR EVOLUTION

To give some overall perspective on the possible direction we are taking as human beings, Appendix E, "How We are Evolving in the New Millennium," is included for your consideration. It offers some interesting viewpoints and guidance for you and the organizations you are part of in considering the desired results you choose to achieve. Please turn to the Appendix and consider the following questions:

What value (insights, learnings) did you receive in reviewing Appendix E?

_____
_____
_____

What is the overall message you get from this suggested evolution of our lives into a whole new world?

_____
_____
_____

## Important Foundational Beliefs

You find yourself very thirsty, but you are in a strange new part of the world. All that is available is a stream of water that you discover in the distance. You run quickly, feeling the expectation of quenching your dry mouth and thirsty body. But as you reach the water, you suddenly have fearful questions, wondering where this water comes from. Is it pure water that is drinkable without getting deathly ill? As the questions are filling your mind, a stranger approaches, one who is very familiar with this area. She explains where the water comes from, that in fact it is safe to drink. You feel yourself trusting her. You drink the cool, fresh water with great passion, finding that your thirst has been satisfied.

In the same way that it was important to know where the water "came from," it is important for you to know and understand the "come from" of the material in *Personal Leadership*, and the beliefs of those who contributed to its creation. By understanding why the title of this book was chosen, you can have greater insight into yourself, and your capacity to maximize the value you receive.

### WORDS

It is the author's sincere desire to not only honor his truths and experiences by using words that are in alignment with his life, but also to use words that honor your values, beliefs, and experiences.

It has been said there are 14,000 definitions to the 500 most commonly used words in the English language, averaging 28 meanings for each word. In reading and working with *Personal Leadership*, change the words you feel uncomfortable with to words that are more appropriate for your beliefs and experiences in life. In doing so you will take responsibility for disregarding or not disregarding the power of any part of the material based on a misunderstanding of words or differences in beliefs. Word definitions unique to *Personal Leadership* are contained in Appendix A, "Concepts and Definitions." Please take a moment to review them.

## Personal Leadership: A Practical Approach for Achieving Individual and Organizational Freedom

All of us, and the organizations we are part of, are constantly seeking freedom to create solutions to challenges, and answers to questions that lead to our desired results. The title of this book was carefully selected to reflect the "come from" of the author.

"Personal"

We can make the choice to provide proactive leadership in all organizations we are a part of, as well as in our own lives, by taking full responsibility to always be learning and growing. In this way, bringing out our very best is a continuous renewal process. When the "critical mass" (this varies with each organization, but usually it's between 40–60 percent) have this attitude, even more powerful results are achieved. The only person any of us can truly change is ourselves.

"Leadership"

This means actively and continuously bringing forth our own individual best efforts and achieving desired results, as individuals and organizations. Leadership is a choice, and not something that is bestowed upon us. Most people hold the paradigm that leadership is for those who have a certain position or responsibility. But "leadership," in the context of this book, means every one of us bringing forth our very best, in every moment, in all that we do. As we do this for ourselves, with others we're associated with, and for each organization we are part of, unprecedented success is realized.

"Practical"

A simple layman's approach with simple words to explain the Principles, Attitudes, and Practices that give us more true freedom, is used to get the essence of the message across. When life is simplified, greater results can be accomplished.

"Achieving"

"The joy of creation (achieving desired results) is one of life's greatest gifts. The joy of creating in companionship (organization) is a treasured adventure." —JENNIFER JOSHUA

"Individual"

Being in touch with our own unique gifts, passions, values, beliefs, attitudes, and desired results is a vital key to personal and organizational success.

"Organization"

Where two or more are united together for a common good cause, whether it's family, community, or business.

"Freedom"

The ability to get desired results more abundantly, easier, and quicker.

## BASIC BELIEFS

### ▶ What is the belief

1. The essence of who we are, is that "we are spiritual beings having a human experience, not humans having a spiritual experience!"

2. Every person in an organization is a leader, with responsibility to contribute their very best each day.

3. The answers to all questions and the solutions to all problems/challenges, as an individual and all organizations we are part of, are within that person and the people of an organization.

4. Resistance to inevitable change is potentially eliminated through a positive focused mind and a physical body willing to learn and grow continuously.

5. The appropriate Principles, Attitudes, and Practices bring freedom (power) to get all the desired results we seek for good.

6. The healthiness of any organization is in direct proportion to the healthiness and contribution of the people that make up the organization.

### ▶ How your freedom for consistently getting the results you seek is increased

1. Knowing who we really are brings us greater capacity to tap into an infinite power that helps us achieve more of what we choose.

2. As each person steps forward and speaks out openly and honestly with their best efforts in contributing to the success of the organization, much more power is available to move that organization successfully forward. Being "right" is not what is needed. What is right for an organization will come forth as people work together, with each one bringing forth what they think and feel.

3. Valuing their people on all levels, and looking to them to contribute beyond what they have been told to do, will increase any organization's success.

4. Resistance blocks success. Helping people heal, grow, and learn to productively and continually contribute to the success of the organization will substantially increase the freedom (power) to accomplish the so-called impossible.

5. There is great power individually and collectively when people choose high ideals and strive to live with integrity to them.

6. As organizations focus attention and resources on their team members, with sincere intent to help them grow and develop, those organizations will naturally draw people who will constantly help accomplish desired results.

## The Call

A man was walking along his own unique path in life. He was fairly comfortable and pleased with all that he had worked so hard for. However, one day he came to a crossroads where he could no longer go in the same direction. He had the choice to go left or right. Going backwards was not acceptable at all. He realized at that moment, the world was thrusting a decision upon him. He could no longer go in the same comfortable direction he had always gone. This caused him to feel very uncomfortable, even fearful. His future felt uncertain. He began to doubt his ability to change directions as the world was forcing him to. "Which path would be the best?" he asked himself. In this confused state, he saw a beautiful old tree. Perched on one of the limbs was an owl. He knew owls were filled with wisdom and so he asked the wise old owl which way he should go.

The wise old owl responded quickly, "It all depends on where you want to go!"

Life does and will bring dramatic changes. You can resist those changes, "check out," or you can practice ways of embracing any and all changes that come your way. We cannot go back. In many ways, we all face an uncertain future. Life is just that way now. Important for thriving in the constant flow of change is being very clear where we and the organizations we are part of are going. What desired results are we after? What are we passionate about?

## The Call

Be clear on the results you seek. Be clear on what you are passionate about in your life. Help every organization you are part of be clear on what it wants. Continuously strive to be the best you can be. Constantly serve yourself and others in balance with the best you can give. Join others in a cause for good and achieve incredible results individually, and within the organizations you commit your efforts and being to.

CHAPTER ONE: GETTING RESULTS

With that in mind, let's make time to pause your life (a concept discussed in detail in Chapter Four) and review the results you and your organizations are seeking. Reflect on how you currently respond to changes in your life, and in the life of the organizations you are part of.

Summarize the results you currently desire to bring into your life (we will refer to these at the end of each section):

_____
_____
_____

Now summarize all the results the organizations you are with are looking to achieve (have a sheet for each "organization" you are a part of):

_____
_____
_____

What is your attitude toward change? How can you flow with change rather than resist it? Do you have a plan to thrive on change?

_____
_____
_____

## Today, By Choice, I Am...

At the end of each chapter, you will be given the opportunity to "power pause" (see Chapter Four) and reflect on what value you have received from going through the preceding material. Take the information that is "truth" for you, and apply it toward actually experiencing it in your every day life. Use this process for making a big difference in getting the results you want. (This concept of knowledge plus experience is discussed in detail in Chapter Four.)

"Today, by choice, I am..." is the beginning of an affirmation statement that will be called your "freedom statement." There is great power in affirmation statements, even though "experts" have mixed opinions about their effect on getting what we want in life. Affirmation statements give clarity, and begin to reprogram the mind into the new paradigms needed for achieving our desired goals and dreams.

Here is an explanation of how there is great power in this beginning phrase:

**Today:**

This takes what you desire from the future into the present, a very important aspect for increasing your freedom to achieve. We need to "act as if" (see Chapter Seven) it were so when we bring in to our lives what is new. *Live from being, not becoming.* This quickens the change and getting results process.

**By Choice:**

Life and what we choose for our lives, is all our *choice.* Adding this word to the affirmation statement brings a greater sense to mind and body of the freedom we enjoy in life, and that we are in control of what we desire.

**I Am:**

There is great power in the words that follow "I am." It is part of taking a stand. It focuses on the present, rather than the past or future. This is another powerful part of quickening the change and getting results process.

Let's look at an example: Say you were inspired by the global vision statement and have chosen to be more in charge of your life than ever before, and you desire to get very clear what you want in your life, or want more of.

Here is a possible "I am" freedom statement:

"Today, by choice, I am completely in charge of my life by daily making clear notes of what it is that I want to be, do, and have in my life."

What will be your "I am" freedom statement to support you getting all that is possible from this book?

Today, by choice, I am…

_____
_____
_____

Take a separate sheet of paper and record all your "I am" statements so you can repeat them over and over. For the greatest effectiveness, "I am" freedom statements should be more than an intellectual exercise. As explained later in this book, when feelings are aroused along with the thoughts (i.e., freedom statements repeated over and over), that is when the greatest power and freedom for achievement comes. Don't be concerned when no feelings come with the repeated affirmation statements. If you repeat your statements slowly, peacefully, and often enough, the feelings will eventually come.

What has been your greatest value from reading this chapter?

_____
_____
_____

Is there something specific that you want more of in your life as a result of this value?

_____
_____
_____

Chapter Three suggests a simple plan for change that can be used to take what you have valued from each chapter into your actual experience in life. Also see Appendix D for a form you can copy for each existing or new result desired.

# 2
# INCREASING YOUR FREEDOM FOR GETTING MORE RESULTS

**How Life Works**

Understanding "what" as presented in this book greatly depends on knowing a practical, uncomplicated approach as to "how" it works. Some may see it as oversimplified. That risk is overshadowed by the impact it will have on you in implementing the "what" (by making sure you understand the "how"). Hopefully, simple and practical is better for you. (Please refer to Appendix A for the book's definition of "energy" before reading further ).

Energy is the unseen force that somehow helps us change, grow, and accomplish what we want in life. There are various ways people choose to put a name to this power. Some include: energy, spirit, love, God, chi, life force, light, the Divine. The words this book uses are "energy," "energy flowing," and "Life." No matter what this force is called, it transcends matter or physical form, and is infinite in its power and supply. In the sports world, they explain this unseen force as "momentum," or "being on a roll."

Let's start with an easy question that most can relate to: What does it feel and look like to be "on a roll"?

_____
_____
_____

Many people who have responded to this question have likely given answers similar to yours. When asked, what is one thing you can always count on happening when "on a roll"?, one typical response is, "it will always end some time or another."

Obviously we can take the opposite of each of your positive responses to give some idea of what it looks and feels like not to be "on a roll." Rather than do that, let's just get to the point!

**"Energy Flowing"**

These two words have been chosen to describe the phenomenon of "being on a roll." There are many other words that could have been selected, but the words aren't the key thing here. It is the essence of understanding momentum that is the real issue.

When you are "on a roll," the energy just seems to flow smoothly and easily and you feel like you could accomplish anything you set your mind to. When you don't feel "on a roll," it feels like nothing seems to work in accomplishing what you want.

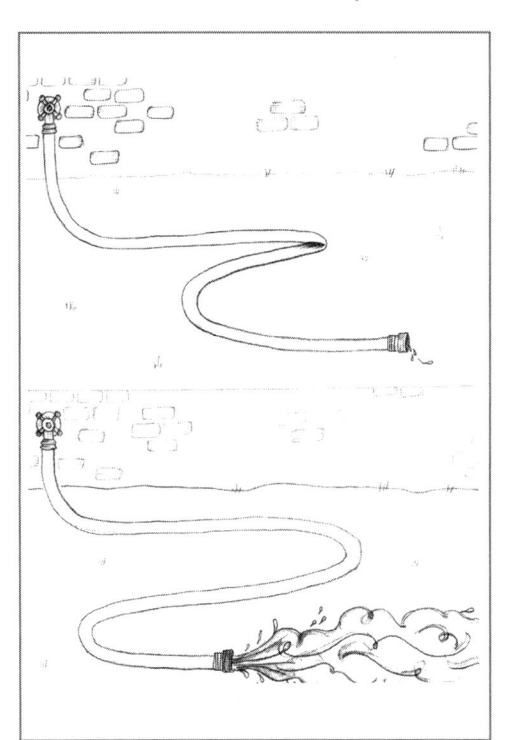

To simplify and clarify this concept, an ordinary garden hose has been chosen as a way to easily see how this phenomenon works. The "garden hose" will be referred to throughout this book, to show how the things presented or shared really work in your everyday life. It will also make implementing (experiencing the full impact of the concepts, Principles, Attitudes, and Practices) much easier.

From our experience in life, we trust that behind this wall there is a huge quantity of water that we can tap into for supplying our needs. For most of us, we have gained such a trust in this water source that we can drink from the garden hose.

The water symbolizes the *source of energy* that is available to help us in all aspects of our life. When positively and repeatedly experienced, we gain great trust in it, just as we have with the water from the garden hose. In reality, this energy supply is much more pure than water, and infinite in supply. It waits for the "demand" (the asking) to have it be real for us in our life.

The faucet symbolizes our *mind* (or in an organization, the mind of all its people), a real key to getting access to this water.

The garden hose symbolizes our *body* (or organization), with the garden hose having a kink in it with little energy flowing through it (top illustration) or the energy is flowing freely and abundantly (bottom illustration). The water coming out is the flow, or lack of flow, of *energy* that helps us get our desired results.

We will discuss throughout the book things that generate that flow, that being "on a roll," and what things "kink" the garden hose (in the mind and body, or in the organization), and how to "unkink" it. We will even talk about how to make the "garden hose" bigger, so that even more water (energy) can flow through it, thus generating even greater power to achieve results more abundantly.

Let's look at these three words: How...Life...Works

## *How*—Simplicity and Practicality

"People resist simplicity because they fear it. A simple idea makes us feel naked, especially when we are surrounded by peers who rely on complexity to mask their ignorance and hedge their bets."
—JACK TROUT, *The Power of Simplicity*

Don't let the simplicity of the material in this book lull you into thinking it doesn't work and you have "heard it before." Those that have embraced these concepts, Principles, Attitudes, and Practices intellectually *and* through their experience, have profited in all levels of their life. And so have the organizations they are part of.

The essence of "how" is very important for this material to have greater impact. Everything presented here is done in the simplest and most practical way possible. Complexity and technical intellectual ramblings about a subject often gets us lost, confused, and makes it easy to give up a good thing.

## *Life*—Being, Doing, Having

You may have tired of the two words "desired results" already. But life, individually and within organizations we are part of, drives us in this focused direction, and more clarity is needed before going further.

Generally speaking, we learn to experience life and then categorize desired results in three areas (Abraham Maslow's famous 1940s "Hierarchy of Needs" is included to help you gain greater clarity on what you choose to accomplish).

19

CHAPTER TWO:
INCREASING YOUR FREEDOM

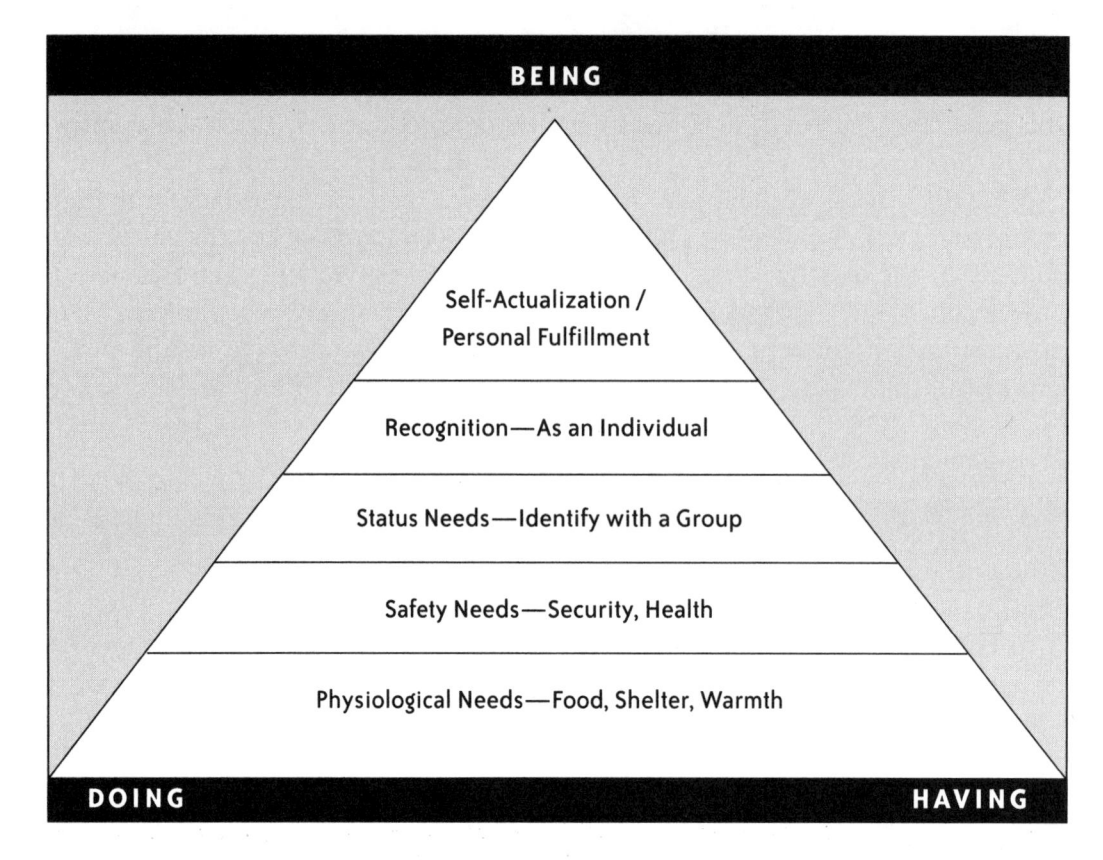

```
                            BEING

                              /\
                             /  \
                            /    \
                           /      \
                          / Self-  \
                         /Actualiza-\
                        /tion/Personal\
                       /  Fulfillment  \
                      /─────────────────\
                     / Recognition—As an \
                    /     Individual      \
                   /───────────────────────\
                  / Status Needs—Identify   \
                 /       with a Group        \
                /─────────────────────────────\
               /  Safety Needs—Security, Health\
              /─────────────────────────────────\
             / Physiological Needs—Food, Shelter,\
            /              Warmth                 \
           /───────────────────────────────────────\
DOING                                                HAVING
```

The purpose of this illustration is to organize our desired results, whether as an individual or an organization, into three main areas:

**Being:**

Who are you? Who do you choose to be? What is your purpose for being? What are the most important values of your character (or the values of your organization) to you. What drives your thoughts, words, and actions? How do you choose to "show up" in the world?

**Doing:**

What do you want to do in your life (for organizations, their mission)? What is your passion? What excites you when you are doing it? How do you choose to serve the world you are in? What contributions do you want to make in your life? What would you like to learn? What gifts or talents would you like to develop? What do you want to accomplish?

**Having:**

What would you like to own? What would you like to experience in life? What do you want to enjoy having? What are your desired results?

### *Works*—Freedom to Get the Results you Want

"Freedom Through Personal Leadership," means that we increase our individual power (and the power in organizations we are part of) to get the results we want by taking personal responsibility in growing and changing in bringing more of the very best we can be. Getting more of the results we seek, and getting them more consistently, is not just about doing more, or just doing things differently; it is finally about who we need to be.

In developing the freedom through personal leadership to achieve desired results, we need to give all three areas (being, doing, having) our full attention, in balance. As stated before, the old paradigm (a mental way one perceives, understands, values, or interprets the world) has been that a lot of hard work (doing) generates the having (desired results). The new millennium is more about being (character, who we are inside/values of organizations), than doing, in order to have.

As Helen Jaspus shared with us: "If all one does is spend their life doing—doing—doing, one ends up in a lot of doo-doo."

Greater freedom begins by being very clear and specific about what results we are looking for in all these areas with a greater focus on the "being" part. Examine the last chapter—how clear were you about your life? How clear were you about what the organizations (remembering that "organizations" is very loosely defined) you are part of want?

### One final thought

Throughout this book the words, "… for the highest good of all," are used. Why is this so important? How does this work with what I want?

To have the full support of this infinite source of energy, life works by law (like the law of gravity; whether we like it or not, it is real and functions regardless of how we want it to be) to make sure that whatever is being sought is what is best for ourselves and for everyone affected by the desired result. It is an important concept to keep in mind because to increase freedom to achieve, this law must be considered and trusted when things do not work out just the way we had planned. When what is being desired is not for our own best good and/or for the best good for others that are affected, then our "garden hose" is "kinked."

Life, or this energy source, has as its purpose to assist *each and all of us* to "be" more of the best we can be, do all that we choose to accomplish, and have all we desire in our lives to enjoy, as we go about our daily lives in service and accomplishment. When the highest goal is not going to happen for ourselves, or for others, this energy is not going to be available to help us nearly as much.

An obvious example is when an organization wants to increase its bottom line financial results and decides to do so illegally. Their human power may gain some results in the short run, but in the long run it will not be consistent, and not as abundant as it could be when the "good for all" is lived by, and is supported by this infinite source of energy.

Pause again and make sure you are clear in the three areas of being, doing, and having: (you may want to turn to Appendix H for suggestions.)

What additional areas do you consider important as to who do you choose to "be"?

_____
_____
_____

What additional things do you want to be doing/accomplishing in your life?

_____
_____
_____

What else do you want to have/enjoy in your life?

_____
_____
_____

The very same questions can be addressed with any organization you are part of. Who are they? What is their mission? (the doing) What desired results do they want?

Now let's pause and apply the "garden hose" concept by looking at things discussed in Chapters One and Two that affect the flow for desired results.

## THE GARDEN HOSE: KINKING VERSUS FLOWING

▶ **"Kinking the Garden Hose"**
(Desired results harder to get)

1. No clarity on desired results.
2. Paralyzed by change.
3. Not wanting to be responsible.
4. Unwilling to change some patterns, beliefs, values, attitudes, thoughts.
5. Unwilling to provide leadership.
6. Resisting major life changes.
7. Criticizes/judges others.
8. Big gap between what one says and what one does.
9. No buy-in to the Divine.
10. Answers/solutions not within self.
11. Unwilling to be our best and give our best in service to others.
12. Unwilling to speak up, openly and honestly.

Add others that come up for you:
_____
_____
_____

▶ **"Energy Flowing"**
(Desired results come easier, quicker, and more abundantly)

1. Clarity on what is desired.
2. Change motivates and enhances continuous improvement.
3. Self-responsibility.
4. Willing to do whatever it takes to achieve desired results.
5. Chooses to provide best for self and all others.
6. Flows with change and makes adjustments.
7. Honors all people and organizations.
8. Gap narrows through self-improvement.
9. Accepts that part of self that is Divine.
10. Trusts the truth that all we need is within ourselves, and for organizations within their people collectively.
11. Chooses to be and give the best within.
12. Gives best thoughts and feelings openly and honestly.

Add others that come up for you:
_____
_____
_____

CHAPTER TWO: INCREASING YOUR FREEDOM

What has been of greatest value to you from reading this chapter?
_____
_____
_____

Is there something specific that you want to add to your desired results because of this value?

_____
_____
_____

Is it worth power pausing now to complete a plan for the added result?
___ Yes ___ No

If yes, copy the Change Master Plan form (page 164) and create your future now.

_____
_____
_____

What will be your "I am" freedom statement to support your plan?

**Today, By Choice, I Am...**

_____
_____
_____
_____

# 3

# A SIMPLE PLAN FOR MANAGING CHANGE AND ACCOMPLISHING MORE

At the end of each chapter you will be invited to change, add to, or delete results you are seeking as recorded in Chapter One and revised in Chapter Two. As part of that process you can create a plan around the insights you have gained. This chapter suggests a systematized approach to organizing your ideas, creating a plan that leads to accomplishing desired results. Appendix D, "Change Master Plan," summarizes this into a form you can copy for each desired result. This plan can be adapted to an individual and to the organizations you are part of.

**1. Be clear.**
   What is the desired result? Put it down in writing, with as much detail as is needed for the mind and body to have a clear picture of what the change looks like (for the mind) and feels like (for the body). Desire is one of the most powerful human forces. It is the fuel to the fires of achievement. Life magnetizes those things around us to bring us what we choose, as long as it is for the good of all.
   Another way to create your vision for yourself or the organization you are part of, is to make a collage or a picture book of all that you choose to be, do, and have. Look for the pictures and words that bring to life your ideal vision. It will have a powerful impact on your ability to get results. It may feel subtle, but it is very real. It's like creating a scrapbook of your future.
   Without clarity of what results (vision, goals, or simply small accomplishments) are desired, and proper planning to support achieving those results, what you experience is left to fate. It would be like the hunter sending his arrow into the woods in hopes that his prey (desired results) will come into the line of fire (life). Not likely!
   It is vitally important to be very clear what you believe. What are the paradigm foundations that consciously and unconsciously drive your thoughts,

feelings/emotions, words, and actions? The word "unconsciously" is used because at times we speak and act certain ways without really being aware of what is driving us to be that way. It just happens. If you are not totally clear about what you believe, look at how you are responding to life, and what is in your life, and the revelations of truth for you will be very clear.

**2. Define motive.**

Write down your answers to these questions, and place them somewhere so that you can get easy access to reading and re-reading them.

Why is the change being made or the chosen results desired?

Is it worth the effort it will take?

This part of the plan is its most important aspect, because your answers are the energizing source to get through difficult moments and conditions.

When change is thrust on you (loss of job, loss of someone close to you, downturn in the economy, change in supply or demand for your product or services) take time to be clear on what you can positively learn from the change and what changes will be needed to successfully move forward (see Chapter Seven, "The Power of One").

When uninvited change comes, answering the motive (why) question may be difficult. But taking time to discuss such a motive is very important in getting through those challenging moments when some form of opposition shows up.

**3. Plan.**

Who will do what, by when. Include what you will do when the emotions come into play, possibly distracting you from your course of actions.

**4. Create "I am..." affirmation statements.**

Read and repeat the statements or record them on an audio cassette and listen as you drive. As often as possible, spend time with these new truths rather than rushing through them in order to check one more thing off your list. Create moments when you can be quiet, peaceful, relaxed, and just spend time seeing what new truth you have created. *Feel* as much as you can, the accomplishment of your "I am" freedom statements in your mind.

**5. Measure your progress.**

How will you know that you are succeeding/have succeeded? Be as specific as possible.

**6. Be aware.**

Choose to consciously watch for every little sign of progress toward the desired results, and celebrate it (see Chapter Ten for the four C's for sustainable growth) in some way. Once you have determined the "what" (desired result), then "Life" will naturally give you the "how" through specific questions you ask. Awareness will then be one of your most important attributes.

**7. Be diligent.**
Review all of the above as often as is needed to keep focused and always progressing. Make it a powerful part of your mental and physical focus throughout the day. *Stay focused!*

**8. Be persistent.**
Always keep going. Sometimes the best way to get past challenges and obstacles is to simply go through them. Keep going no matter what feedback you are getting internally or externally. Here are some suggestions to use with the affirmation statements you have created:
- Write it down in detail.
- Say it out loud a few times to make sure it feels powerful to you, with the words that evoke positive and powerful feelings.
- Record it and listen to it frequently. Baroque music in the background accelerates the learning process and helps the receptivity process of the mind and body.
- Visualize it as if it were accomplished, bringing in as many feelings in the accomplishment as possible.
- Keep belief in the truth high, disregarding any doubts or fears.

"Genius is only the power of making continuous efforts.
The line between failure and success is so fine
that we scarcely know when we pass it;
so fine that we are often on the line and do not know it.
How many a man (woman) has thrown up his (her) hands at a time
when a little more effort, a little more patience,
would have achieved success.
As the tide goes out, so it comes in.
In business, sometimes, prospects may seem darkest
when really they are on the turn.
A little more persistence, a little more effort,
and what seemed hopeless failure
may turn to glorious success.
There is no failure except in no longer trying.
There is no defeat except from within,
no really insurmountable barrier
save our own inherent weakness of purpose." —ELBERT HUBBARD

### 9. Let go.

When the illusion of failure comes, feel any negative feelings for a moment. Observe these feelings without judgment, then let them go into the wind, never to return. Do this no matter how many times failure shows up. *No matter how many times!*

### 10. Decide accountability.

Who will you share your desired results with (see "Stewardship and Accountability" in Chapter Four) that can help you along the way to get what you want? When will you consistently report back to them?

### 11. Adjust plan.

As you progress towards succeeding with your accomplishments, there will always be the need to continually adjust your original plan. Remain flexible. Remain aware. When you have reached some level of success, it may be very important to let go of part or all of the old plan and make way for what's next.

### 12. Celebrate.

When the result has been achieved, have a formal or short informal celebration. Be playful with this. It will enhance future changes and results achieved because celebration and play increases the energy to accomplish. It really works! As part of this process, determine what specific things you did that led to your success. Use these learnings for future change.

**Special note of importance:** Life seems to always give us what we desire (or better!), as long as it is in our best good, and the best good for all. At first, success may not be the end result. Success may be in all the learnings that have come along your path. So keep going—and enjoy the journey!

## RESISTANCE

Resistance is a normal human reaction to various aspects of our lives, whether it be in thoughts, feelings/emotions, words or actions. It's important to the results getting process to handle resistance in ways that keep you moving forward and "staying on a roll."

Resisting change "kinks" the flow of energy. The form of this resistance can take varies. Some examples are:

- Something happens in your life that you did not want to happen and you are angry or fearful.

- You know you need to change something about yourself but you are frustrated by your seeming lack of power to do so.
- You verbally complain about the recent changes that are made by your company.
- You wish your life were different.
- You don't want to work for what you choose to have in your life.
- You don't like the long commute to work and complain about it.
- You don't want to give that talk to a group.

What other areas of your life are you now seeing some form of resistance in?

_____
_____
_____

Resistance can be a very subtle thing. But it has an enormous power to "kink the garden hose" and restrict your freedom to accomplish desired results. Accepting what life brings, in all forms, and staying open to what you are to gain and learn from all things that occur in your life, will keep you open to the energy flow. You get through, faster and easier, that which you are resisting, and get the results you really want. Acceptance is a very high form of self love, and love for others.

Pause for a moment and reflect now on what things you have learned, or been reminded of that either "kink the garden hose" or open it up for more flow for supporting you in your achievements. Some have been suggested here, and as in all the chapters, there is space to evaluate what you have read toward your understanding of how life works. Appendix C, "Things That Affect the Flow for Desired Results," has a summarized list for additional reference.

Accepting the plan outlined in this chapter is *not* what is important. However, the concept is. You may want to take time now to create your own unique plan around change. Having a plan is vital for increasing the quantity, quality, and timeliness of accomplishing what you want.

Is there something specific that you want to add to your desired results (what results as well as how to get them)?

_____
_____
_____

## THE GARDEN HOSE: KINKING VERSUS FLOWING

▶ **"Kinking the Garden Hose"**
(Desired results harder to get)

1. Attitude: Being "on a roll" will end.
2. Resisting life (or parts of it).
3. Complexity.
4. No plan around change.
5. Not clear on why you want the results you seek.
6. What is wanted is not for everyone's best good.

Add others that come up for you:
_____
_____
_____

▶ **"Energy Flowing"**
(Desired results come easier, quicker, and more abundantly)

1. Attitude: I am always "on a roll."
2. Accepting what life brings.
3. Simplicity.
4. Identifying and using a plan to adapt to change.
5. Clear and motivated by why you have chosen what you have to achieve.
6. Always adding the words "for the highest good for all" to your desires.

Add others that come up for you:
_____
_____
_____

What has been of greatest value to you from reading this chapter?
_____
_____
_____

Is there something specific that you want to add to your desired results because of this value?
_____
_____
_____

Is it worth power pausing now to complete a plan for the added result?
___ Yes ___ No

If yes, copy the Change Master Plan form (page 164) and create your future now.

_____
_____
_____

What will be your "I am" freedom statement to support your plan?

**Today, By Choice, I Am...**

_____
_____
_____
_____
_____

# 4
# FIVE KEY CONCEPTS FOR ENHANCING PERSONAL LEADERSHIP

## Knowledge Plus Experience

Most people are experts at acquiring more knowledge and information. This expertise is a vital ingredient to our progress. *Personal Leadership* has, as its cornerstone, doing whatever it takes to *apply* this knowledge to everyday living, and to experience more fully the desired results.

Personal leadership in the new millennium is about taking the time and making the effort to really apply the knowledge/insights we gain, so that we are always increasing our power to bring out the very best that is within us in service to people and organizations.

There is a dramatic difference in the results you can achieve by experiencing the freedom gained from truth through application, versus just acquiring more information, knowledge/truth.

What does this sentence mean to you?

_____
_____
_____

Some researchers state that 99 percent of all people are great at acquiring information, but are not good at, or even interested in, gaining the wisdom from that information by applying it.

The phrase, "And ye shall know the truth, and the truth shall make you free" is often taken out of context (in terms of personal leadership development) for achieving personal or organizational goals and results. Ignorance, of course, blocks our progress. But truth is only half learned (in reality it is far less than 50 percent in terms of achieving results) if we do not take the time and give the attention and focus to experience in our body the effects of any truth we have gained. For example, the truth may be that you need to lose five pounds. But until the body supports that decision and does its part (exercise, eating healthier), the desired result will not be achieved.

Another lesson from life that emphasizes this point is in the public speaking industry. We frequently hear the comment that we teach what we have to learn. These public speakers are fantastic at expressing truth, but have a difficult time implementing it into their own lives. Because of the essence of its purpose, the new millennium will naturally cause a greater alignment with what we say and what we do.

What is the difference? Rather than tell you (where only the mind is involved) the difference, let's experience (where the body is involved) the difference for ourselves. This can be illustrated with a short game.

Here is a simple statement of truth: By applying some simple rules, you will dramatically increase your success from the first time playing the following game to the second. You will play the game twice, once without rules and the second time with rules.

The next page is full of numbers. Connect with a continuous line as many consecutive numbers together as possible in 60 seconds, beginning with number 1, then 2, and so on. Your line may go through other numbers, but you must go from 1 to as high as you can in 60 seconds with consecutive numbers.

Now turn to the next page and begin (for 60 seconds).

CHAPTER FOUR: FIVE KEY CONCEPTS

34

PERSONAL
LEADERSHIP

What number did you reach _____?

Before turning to the next page to play the game for the second time, here are some simple instructions.

1. Draw two lines on the next page of numbers by dividing the sheet into quarters. One vertical line divides the page in half vertically, and another line divides the page in half horizontally.
2. Write "odd" in the upper left column and "even" in the upper right column.
3. All of the odd numbers are on the left side of the paper, and all of the even numbers are on the right side of the page.
4. The sequence of every six numbers rotate between the upper half of the page and the lower half of the page. For example: 1–6 are in the top half, 7–12 are in the bottom half, 13–18 are in the top half, and 19–24 are in the bottom half.

Now turn the page over and do it again (for 60 seconds), following these guidelines.

36

PERSONAL LEADERSHIP

What number did you reach this time? _____

Most people realize a significant increase in their results. How do you feel about your success?

_____
_____
_____

If by chance you did not score higher, don't be discouraged. There are many factors involved in getting to a higher number the second time, but the lesson here is that it is one thing to be told you will have greater success, and quite another to experience the difference and feel in the body what has been achieved.

By applying the concepts, Principles, Attitudes, and Practices contained in this book, you will begin to feel an increase in your true freedom. The only way to know if what is promised is true is to apply what you feel is important from this book and to experience the difference, just like in this game. You will have a choice to either learn the things presented here or to learn *and apply* them day after day until they become a natural part of you. The difference in the results you achieve in life will be dramatically greater through application and practice, and you will realize greater results much easier and quicker than before.

What value did you get from this concept of acquiring knowledge versus gaining experience? Does it have real meaning to you? If you value this concept what specifically will you do more of, better, or differently in your life for accomplishing more of your desired results?

_____
_____
_____
_____
_____

## Power Pausing

Consistently take off the "roller skates" of life!

There are innumerable benefits when this concept is applied. Everyday life is so fast-paced and we are pushed right along with it, unless we choose to not be in such a hurry all the time and stop to focus on the things that matter most in our lives. This concept is just as applicable in an organization as it is to each of us personally.

Because of this rapid pace of life and the changes thrust on us, we become like the person in a car, waiting for the light to change, so we can quickly speed off to our next destination, or thing to do.

Power pausing has a wide range of applications. It may be as simple as taking deep breaths five to ten times a day where you can evaluate if what you are doing and thinking is in alignment with your desired results. Review your desired results each morning and evening, feeling each time what their accomplishment would feel like. As Richard Eyre says, "Awareness is the source of joy." It is also the source of achieving desired results easier and quicker.

For your reference, see Appendix J, "Twelve Areas of Balance," Appendix K, "Preparing Your Personal Life Plan," and also Appendix L, "Vision for Organizations." They are given to be helpful in your pausing time.

Power pausing may initially take hours or days (even a week or two) if you have not given much thought to your desired results. Organizations typically take substantial amounts of time creating and adjusting their vision, mission, and strategies. An individual certainly can create that much value and more, and taking time to get clear is absolutely paramount.

## Spend Time with Truth

Nurture and love truth as you would a child. Be quiet with truth; let it be absorbed in your body as it is in your mind. Get a sense of how you will apply it so that truth is fully learned and applied and assists you in your achievements. Visualize and/or write with clarity on your new truth, and see and feel its impact on your life. Pausing and taking precious time with the things we sense are really important for our lives cannot be emphasized enough. The most significant way to gain our own testimony is to go from truth as an idea to our actually experiencing it, until it becomes a natural new pattern for each of us.

What value does this concept have for you?

_____
_____
_____

What will be your plan to implement a pausing program that is worthy of the goals and results you have chosen?

_____
_____
_____

How will you contribute to the organizations you are a part of with this powerful concept?

_____
_____
_____

## Stewardship and Accountability

Stewardship and accountability are significant concepts in accomplishing our chosen results easier and quicker in our lives, and the success of our organizations. Why? Simply due to our human nature. Generally speaking, we change after pain is felt or something has "gone wrong," and we seem to slide or "tread water" when things are easy and good. Unfortunately, we tend to be driven by fear, rather than love.

Stewardship and accountability help us to be more proactive and progressive. Stewardship is having a clear understanding of your specific role and responsibilities for your own life and in all the organizations you are part of. This comes by having agreements as to what these roles and responsibilities are. For example, as a parent, your stewardship is defined by your own beliefs and the beliefs of your spouse, and the agreements you make with each other as to how to raise your children. As an employee, your stewardship is mostly defined by the company and your supervisor with the job you were hired for. Having clarity in great detail will better help you be aware of just what your stewardship is, so that you know what results you are expected to generate. The ideal performance evaluation is when a person's stewardship is so clear and well-communicated that when the evaluation is held, it is mostly a self-evaluation because things were so clear up front that it is obvious when results have been satisfactorily achieved. To be accountable, we must be clear with all that we are responsible for.

It is important to understand all the areas of stewardship in our lives. Being clear what this means in the organizations you are a part of is very important to being successful. What are your responsibilities, in detail? How will you know you are successful? Clear communications in this area are a must.

Then comes the next challenge. The old paradigm judged us as "wrong" when things did not go as planned, and the expected results did not quite happen. Blame was placed. Maybe fear and control was used to manipulate. When the word accountability is used, normally negative feelings can be aroused. But it takes a special kind of leadership to make accountability be effective.

"When performance is measure, performance improves.
When performance is measured and reported back,
Performance is accelerated."
—THOMAS S. MONSON

1. How do we provide stronger leadership for getting desired changes/results without all the negativity?

By shifting our attitude about accountability. Accountability is an opportunity to live by choice rather than by accident. Accountability assists in generating desired results, faster. Our success in life becomes more proactive and creative. We become life, rather than letting it pass us by. Transformation is created more consistently. It generates sustainability of change. Transformation lives in accountability. Accountability is a positive thing with the right leadership.

2. What is the most appropriate leadership for creating a positive environment around the accountability process?
- Ask the one being held accountable!
- Here are some possible questions to ask: How best do I support you when you succeed? How best do I support you when you fall short?
- Come to a mutual agreement with how success is measured and what the consequences are for not doing what is agreed upon.
- Agree on a regular time to meet to review progress.
- Be sincere in giving love, support, and acceptance.
- Keep communications open and honest, and share thoughts and feelings calmly. Agree that "telling the truth as fast as you can" is desired.
- Have clear intentions for the accountability process. Suggestions would be:
    Help to stay focused.
    Assess when to take risks.

Accelerate success.
Assist in pushing through any and all obstacles that may arise.
Keep motivation high.
Measure progress.
Determine where support is needed.
A deep and sincere caring for the one accountable.
Belief in the person's capacity to succeed.

What has been the highest value to you from this concept?
_____
_____
_____

Is this value worth pausing now to make sure when and how you will implement it?
____ Yes ____ No

If yes, pause and plan:
_____
_____
_____

## Sharing Experiences

The great success of the "Chicken Soup" series of books give us tangible evidence of the power of sharing experiences with those who have similar desires to improve their lives. In our personal lives, it is very helpful to find someone, hopefully more than one, to share learnings.

Organizations see a dramatic increase in the energy/momentum in their people when permission is given to share success stories. Such experiences open people up to learn and apply truth more quickly. Results are achieved easier and faster. We all become mentors to each other! A simple weekly brown bag lunch, or even a lunch provided by the organization, can have a significant impact on the progress of the company.

By sharing your experience with someone, it deepens and strengthens your own experience and quickens the results you continue to want more of. Stories take theory into real life applications.

### THE GARDEN HOSE: KINKING VERSUS FLOWING

▶ **"Kinking the Garden Hose"**
**(Desired results harder to get)**

1. Fast paced life.
2. Never completely stopping.
3. Learning without applying.
4. Life drives you.

Add others that come up for you:
_____
_____
_____

▶ **"Energy Flowing"**
**(Desired results come easier, quicker, and more abundantly)**

1. Slowing down.
2. Pausing frequently.
3. Applying what is learned that will make a difference.
4. Principle-centered, attitude-driven, practice-committed.

Add others that come up for you:
_____
_____
_____

What has been of greatest value to you from reading this chapter?

_____
_____
_____

Is there something specific that you want to add to your desired results because of this value?

_____
_____
_____

Is it worth power pausing now to complete a plan for the added result?
___ Yes ___ No

If yes, copy the Change Master Plan form (page 164) and create your future now.

_____
_____
_____

What will be your "I am" freedom statement to support your plan?

**Today, By Choice, I Am…**

_____
_____
_____
_____

CHAPTER FOUR: FIVE KEY CONCEPTS

# 5

# THE POWER OF BEING PRINCIPLE-CENTERED, ATTITUDE-DRIVEN, AND PRACTICE-COMMITTED

### The Link between Principles, Attitudes, and Practices

There is a very powerful linkage between your chosen Principles, Attitudes, and Practices, and the quality and quantity of results that you achieve.

To understand this linkage, return to the illustration in Chapter Two (page 20) that described the areas of results: being, doing, and having. These three areas correlate directly to what makes up our whole being.

Each of us has a body, a mind, and the Divine (see Appendix A for definition). The Divine part of us would like us to be all that we possibly can be in terms of a noble character. The mind wants to do, do, do, based on long to-do lists, need to learn, etc. The body wants to have things, experience life, and have fun. Note that Abraham Maslow's hierarchy of needs (page 20) follows right along with this. The Divine seeks self-actualization and personal fulfillment. The mind needs recognition as an individual, and status as an identity with a group. The body needs safety, security, and health, and physiological needs of food, shelter, and warmth.

Before we link Principles, Attitudes, and Practices to the Divine, mind, and body, let's discuss each part in more depth.

### Mind, Body, and the Divine

Our full capacity—mentally, physically, and spiritually—has been relatively untapped. These three parts of our whole being can be brought together into more harmony and balance in order for each of us to accomplish things never before experienced, results that in the past have been achieved by a few "dynamic leaders." This will happen to all of us who are willing to accept the call and step toward our full potential individually and collectively.

Although experts conclude through tangible evidence that the power of the mind is beyond our understanding, the power of the body, even to heal itself and go past the sensation of pain, is just now being realized by the "average" person. The Divine is an infinite source of energy in each of us, "Life" force—a source for all that we need for our unique journey here on earth.

Since the mind is the key link in uniting the Divine with our physical bodies, we will spend significant time reviewing some basic concepts about how the mind works in simple and practical terms.

"We are just beginning to discover the virtually limitless capacities of the mind." —DR. JEAN HOUSTON

"We will, by conscious command, evolve cerebral centers which will permit us to use powers that we now are not even capable of imagining."
—DR. FREDRIC TILNIZ

"The ultimate creative capacity of the brain may be, for practical purposes, infinite."
—DR. RICHARD LEAKEY

"We are at the point of developing talents we haven't got words for."
—PATRICIA SUN, *psychologist*

## HOW TO MAKE A DIFFERENCE IN HOW MUCH WE SUCCEED AT GETTING DESIRED RESULTS

This illustration emphasizes in a dramatic but real way, the greater power in achieving results when integrating the Divine level with the mind and body, rather than relying on the doing (mind) level and having (body) level. Much more is available when all three parts are united, aligned, and working together.

The size of the funnel opening symbolizes the quantity and quality of results we can get. Which end would you choose?

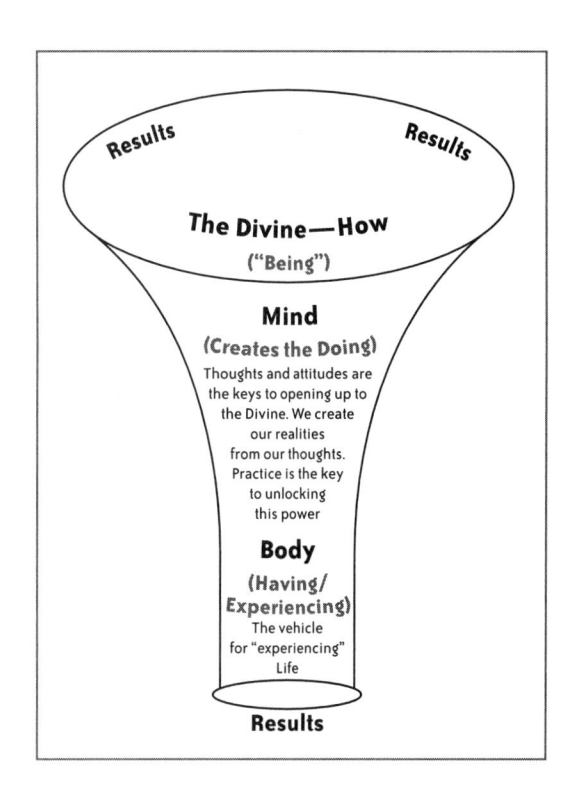

## OUR MINDS

> "The empires of the future are empires of the mind."
> —WINSTON CHURCHILL

A researcher in Virginia came up with the following finding: If all the hydrogen atoms in our minds could be harnessed, the power produced would light up the whole United States for six months. That power would be worth 200 billion dollars.

From the neck down, we are worth a couple hundred dollars a week. From the neck up, our worth is at least 200 billion dollars.

What are you willing to accept as truth about the capacity and importance of your mind? Pause and sincerely answer this question.

_____
_____
_____

> "Mind is the Master power that molds and makes,
> And Man is Mind, and evermore he takes
> The tool of Thought, and shaping what he wills,
> Brings forth a thousand joys, a thousand ills—
> He thinks in secret, and it comes to pass:
> Environment is but his looking-glass."
> —JAMES ALLEN

Power pause now and reflect on what James Allen shares with us. Also, record what effect, if any, this quote can have on your life, and on your ability to achieve what you want to be, to do, and to have in your life.

_____
_____
_____

What does James Allen suggest when he shares "Environment is but his looking-glass"?

_____
_____
_____

Every single thought has an impact on our life, however small that impact is. However, thoughts that are consistently held in the mind, have a powerful and significant impact. The world around us (conditions and circumstances) and in us (our health and emotions) is a true reflection of what is going on in our mind. All this suggests that if we want to change our world, we begin by changing our thoughts, our inner world!

This also suggests that all of our actions and behaviors ("plants" that grow in the gardens of our lives) come from hidden seeds of thought. Our thoughts are like a garden. When no control over our thoughts occurs, then "weeds" grow in the garden, and the garden runs wild with whatever is in the ground. Our lives become controlled by the winds, blowing us here and there.

We cannot expect to plant tomato seeds for getting corn. In others words, thoughts (mind) of fear will not bring about acts (body) of courage. What seeds we plant is what we will get. Plant corn seeds and we get stalks of corn. If you want an abundance of money in your life, you can't expect that to happen if your thoughts and actions are filled with lack, fear, and greed.

> "By the right choice and true application of thought, man (woman) ascends to the Divine perfection; by the abuse and wrong application of thought, he/she descends below the level of the beast. Between these two extremes are all the grades of character, and man (woman) is their maker and master.
>
> "…man (woman) is the master of thought, the molder of character, and the maker and shaper of condition, environment, and destiny."
> —JAMES ALLEN

**REVOLUTIONARY OR EVOLUTIONARY CHANGE?**

Revolutionary: A complete change over a short period of time.
Evolutionary: A process over a sustained period of time of development or change.

Which will be your approach to change for bringing and keeping those thoughts that will create more of your chosen results?

_____
_____
_____

CHAPTER FIVE: THE POWER OF BEING PRINCIPLE-CENTERED

When you take time to pause and reflect on the current conditions in your life and decide which Principles your being is going to establish, you truly become the captain of your ship, directing your energies with great power through thoughts and actions that support those Principles. This is true individually, and for organizations.

Only then are we able to stay aware of what is going on from day to day, adjust the course as needed, and enjoy the incredible experience of achieving the things we desire. We will utilize everything that happens to us for our betterment.

> "Man (woman) is buffeted by circumstances so long as he (she) believes himself (herself) to be the creature of outside conditions, but when he (she) realizes that he (she) is a creative power, and that he (she) may command the hidden soil and seeds of his (her) being out of which circumstances grow, he (she) then becomes the rightful master of himself (herself)... Circumstance does not make the man (woman); it reveals him (her) to himself (herself)." —JAMES ALLEN

What goes on within an organization is an accumulation of people's thoughts. No wonder communications, buy-in, and alignment are important practices within any organization.

One final thought from James Allen: "Let a man (woman) radically alter his (her) thoughts, and he (she) will be astonished at the rapid transformation it will affect in the material conditions of his (her) life. Men (women) imagine that thought can be kept secret, but it cannot; it rapidly crystallizes into habit, and habit solidifies into circumstances."

Obviously, we do have control over our circumstances, but this control is through our thoughts, not what we choose as conditions in our life. How do you now feel about your mind, and the capacity and control it has over achieving your desired results?

_____
_____
_____

## The Capacity of the Human Mind

Now let's give full attention to our mind. Enlightened Leadership International shares with us that there are three focus factors of the mind:

1. We can only focus on one thing at a time.
2. Avoiding doesn't work.
3. We get more of what we focus on.

Take time to pause and be very clear with the profound significance of these three aspects of the mind.

*We can only focus on one thing at a time.* What significance does this concept of the mind have on your life?

Personally:

_____
_____
_____

Within Your Organizations:

_____
_____
_____

If we can only focus on one thing at a time, it is paramount that we *actively choose* what we focus on. Otherwise we are at the mercy of what life brings us and what just comes up in our mind.

*Avoiding doesn't work.* The mind simply does not process and the body does not function on words like "don't." It actually draws us to do what we don't want. Resistance to something is like a magnet! "Don't" is a resistance word.
Examples:
1. Have you ever said to yourself "don't overeat," and then find yourself unable to achieve the result you wanted?
2. A true story: A famous football player focused on "do not throw interceptions." In the key game of the year, he threw an interception in the final minutes to lose the game.
3. In the national drug campaign did you notice that they went from "Don't do drugs" (which would lead to the opposite desired behavior) to "Just say no"?

Many organizations have "don't" throughout their training manuals, policy and procedures manuals, and even in vision, mission, and goal statements. What significance does this concept of the mind have on your life?

Personally:

_____
_____
_____

Within Your Organizations:

_____
_____
_____

Always try to re-state negative to positive. Instead of "zero defects," say "100 percent accuracy." Real experiences of people throughout the world have proven that results are dramatically better and quicker when this change has been implemented.

*You get more of what you focus on.* What a powerful truth! What significance does this aspect of the mind have on your life?

Personally:

_____
_____
_____

Within Your Organizations:

_____
_____
_____

In the absence of the positive results you want in your life, your mind will revert to avoiding what you don't want! Because we are fed so much negative information through newspapers, magazines, Internet, and television, the mind will naturally focus on the negative.

## THE BODY

The body is the vehicle of the mind and the Divine. It is the literal creation of them both. In other words, our physical bodies, along with our conditions and circumstances in life, reveal to us the thoughts we consistently hold and the principles and values we guide our lives by. The Divine honors the agency of the mind so much that whatever the mind chooses, it is reflected in our words and actions. When mind can be aligned with the Divine, then real magic in terms of who we can be, what we can do, and what we have, occurs with unexpected success.

> "If one advances confidently (an attitude of the mind) in the direction of his (her) dreams (a creation of the mind, body, and possibly the Divine), and endeavors to live the life which he (she) has imagined (the mind), he (she) will meet with a success unexpected in common hours...."
> —HENRY DAVID THOREAU

If the mind constantly feeds the body negative thoughts, then disease and ill health occur. Scientists have proven that most of our health or illness is a result of our accumulated thinking patterns. Fear thoughts are more likely to kill a person than bullets or accidents.

> "Anxiety quickly demoralizes the whole body, and lays it open to the entrance of disease; while impure thoughts, even if not physically indulged, will soon shatter the nervous system."   —JAMES ALLEN

If this is true for you, what is your body revealing to you about your current thought patterns?

_____
_____
_____

The body can be the doormat of thoughts walking all over it, or the doorway to great accomplishments. The body is a delicate and pliable vehicle that clearly is driven by the mind. Where your body takes you is totally in the control of your mind. Where the mind stays, the body goes!

> "All that a man (woman) achieves and all that he (she) fails to achieve is the direct results of his (her) own thoughts."   —JAMES ALLEN

CHAPTER FIVE: THE POWER OF BEING PRINCIPLE-CENTERED

When you combine thought with high standards of choice, beliefs, vision, principles, attitudes, practices, and dreams, all things literally become possible! Drifting or just "treading water" in life will not get you the results you desire.

To summarize:
1. Define major purpose(s).
2. Decide thoughts to support purpose.
3. Constantly focus thoughts.
4. Resolve to persist no matter how many times so-called "failure" shows up.
5. Trust that the energy to accomplish the desired goals is being generated.
6. Remain infinite in who you can be, what you can do, and what you can have to enjoy.

## Feelings and Emotions in Personal Leadership

"Thoughts, as powerful as they are, and expectations, create such a small place for God to flow through. But... experiencing and feeling... now that creates limitlessness."   —SARAH PETERSON

What does this mean to you?

_____
_____
_____

Feelings and emotions are more powerful than anything else in terms of generating energy for accomplishing results. They can dramatically enhance your freedom, or they can stop you in your tracks and restrict your freedom. They can be created, or emerge within the body without any warning. Something in the outer world seems to just trigger them. They can become out of control at times, depending on the circumstances and your background.

Strong opinions arise around matters of abuse. Whether verbal or physical, abuse normally occurs without a person's permission, making them truly victims. All abuse is horrible in nature, and its origins are very complex to understand. If you or others in the organizations you are part of have real issues with abuse, it is best not to deal with it directly. Seek help from professionals and the Divine.

Generally speaking, there are four potential harmful emotions that humans deal with:
Anger
Guilt
Fear
Insecurity

Chapter Seven, "The Power of One," reviews some guidelines for working together as teams. Some of what is presented there also applies to getting assistance from others in dealing with these emotions.

Here are some very general suggestions for dealing with very strong, freedom restricting emotions within yourself, and/or with others:

Allow the emotion to come up. Restrain yourself from judging it as bad or wrong, whether with yourself or someone else. A judgmental reaction (toward yourself or toward others you associate with) can inflame the emotion even more. The emotion is okay as long as the outward expression is not doing harm to someone else.

Let yourself, or the person with the high emotion, experience it fully on an internal level. Don't ignore or bury it. Burying difficult emotions eventually leads to poor physical health. Ask positive focused questions (what am I to learn from this?) that may reveal what is triggering the feelings, and why the intensity is there.

Stay at choice! Before acting out (the first sign an internal emotion could lead to outer expression), choose to remain positive focused. It is a learning opportunity for everyone involved if this attitude is maintained and everyone stays open. It can be an excellent opportunity to break through patterns that no longer serve you in getting the results you and others choose. Making new choices on what to do with these emotions is supported by following the four C's for sustainable growth presented in Chapter Ten.

Ultimately, it may take surrendering the emotions to the Divine, because there just may not be a worldly solution to what you or others have experienced.

Openness is a key, as long as you get helpful support in the process.

Balance is another key. There are times when stopping and taking a break is what is needed. Having the intent to hang in there and learn and grow can be sustained so that separation is not the solution.

Let Go! Learning how to let go of these harmful feelings and emotions is an important tool to learn and experience. Many people find it helpful to play with this. For example, see the emotion as a butterfly each time it

CHAPTER FIVE:
THE POWER OF BEING PRINCIPLE-CENTERED

comes up and see it fly away. Some even thank it for coming up and for no longer staying in the body.

Anger, guilt, fear, and insecurity generate zero energy levels. They are termed negative or dark emotions. But in reality, they simply block the flow of Divine energy, like a dam blocks the water from the mountains and creates a reservoir. However, this reservoir can create some very harmful effects on the physical body. This whole area is very complex. Experienced individuals who work with energy in relationships can be supportive, and also help facilitate healing.

The more fun side of feelings are the ones created from our thoughts and imagination. When positive thoughts and positive feelings are combined, great energy is generated, and that leads to our achieving more, faster.

Another suggestion with difficult emotions is to see yourself in the middle of the emotions you are choosing to change. See and feel yourself move quickly through them to the positive feelings you are choosing. Practice this over and over again, and your power to overcome the four harmful emotions is greatly enhanced, increasing your freedom for getting results. Feel the feelings of victory when you are practicing. Acknowledge your mind and body for accomplishing this great thing. You will be amazed when your old patterns have no strength, or have completely gone away.

*The key to all feelings and emotions is to remain at the point of choice.* Choose what you want. Choose not to act out when in the middle of a harmful emotion. Choose to practice in your mind getting what you want. Choose to not be a victim, but one who is in control of your feelings. Choose to accept yourself and others for being okay as you and they are, so that the process of change can be easier and faster. Resisting and judging yourself or others for these harmful emotions only deepens their roots in our minds and bodies.

## Keys to Learning Through the Mind and Body

The following graphs show the importance of repetition. The more we learn through experience, what we learn is more powerful and long lasting, and stays with us to direct our efforts. But in the process of learning, there is some interesting research available to us.

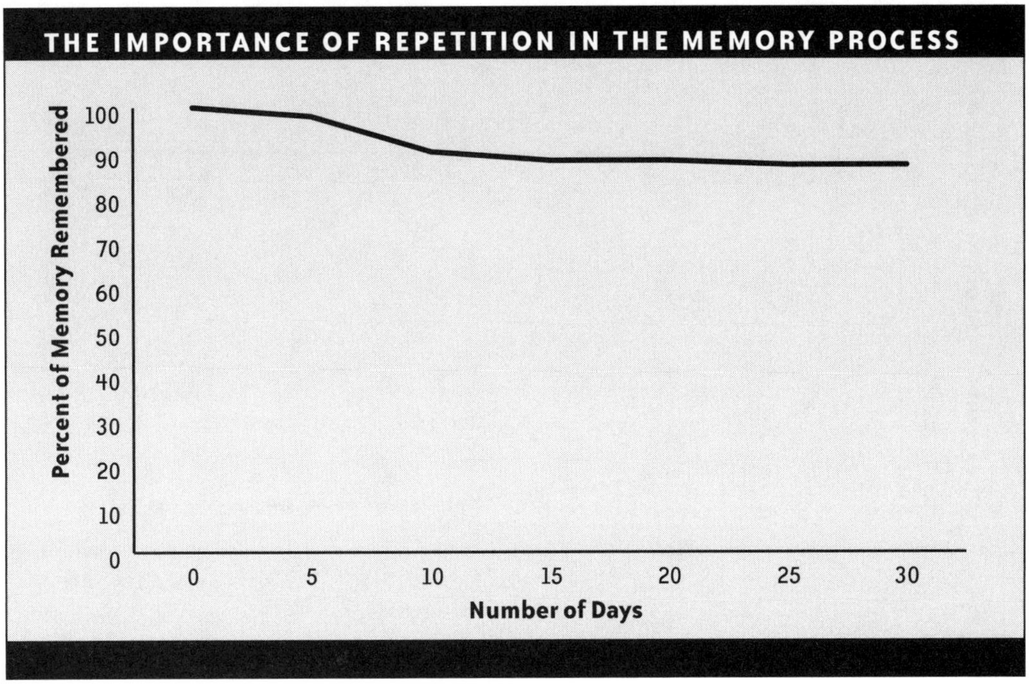
THE IMPORTANCE OF REPETITION IN THE MEMORY PROCESS
Percent of Memory Remembered
100
90
80
70
60
50
40
30
20
10
0
0
5
10
15
20
25
30
Number of Days



> "A message read or heard several times a day for eight days is virtually memorized. At the end of 30 days the memory retains 90 percent of the message." —RESEARCH BY HERMAN EBBINGHAUS

What significance does the graph and the quote have for you?

________________________________________________________________

________________________________________________________________

________________________________________________________________

## LACK OF REPETITION IN THE MEMORY PROCESS

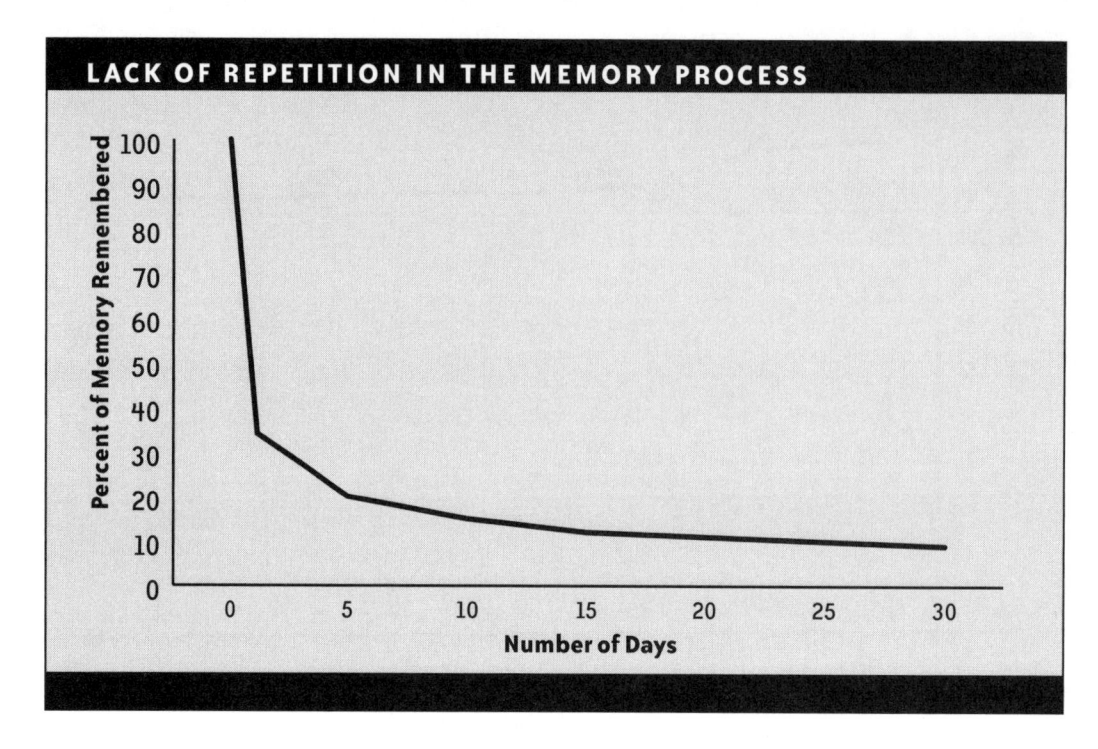

*"A message read or heard only once is 66 percent forgotten within 24 hours and is practically out of the mind in 30 days."*
—RESEARCH BY HERMAN EBBINGHAUS

What significance does the graph and the quote have for you?

_____
_____
_____

We remember/learn:
- A. 10% of what we read
- B. 20% of what we hear
- C. 30% of what we see
- D. 50% of what we see and hear
- E. 70% of what is discussed
- F. 80% of what is experienced*
- G. 95% of what we teach!

*Experts tell us that the body very often cannot tell the difference between something imagined and something actually experienced. Visualization is very helpful in the "business" of getting results.

## TYPES OF LEARNING

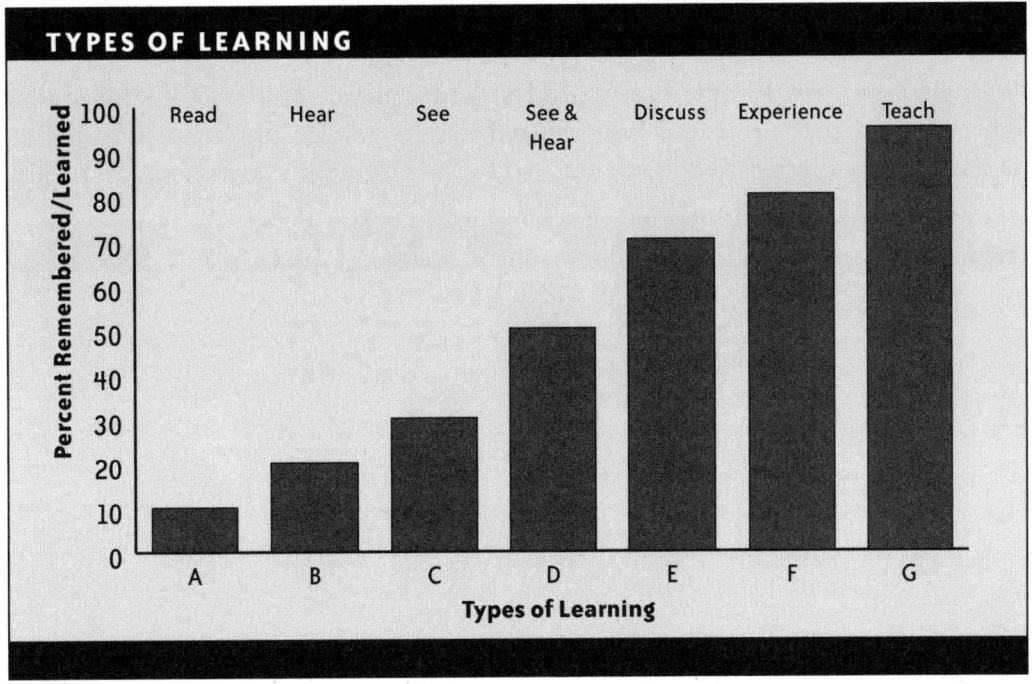

| Type | Label | Percent Remembered/Learned |
|------|-------|---------------------------|
| A | Read | 10 |
| B | Hear | 20 |
| C | See | 30 |
| D | See & Hear | 50 |
| E | Discuss | 70 |
| F | Experience | 80 |
| G | Teach | 95 |

What significance does the graph and "message from the experts" have for you?

_____
_____
_____

Thoughts are the doorway that opens us to a whole new world of possibility. When our bodies actually experience truth, and all the feelings that go with that experience, real power to accomplish is fully realized (see Chapter Two).

## The Divine

The essence of the Divine obviously varies from person to person. For those who believe in a source greater than themselves, with infinite resources for our lives, there is much to learn, experience, apply, and enjoy. From the author's perspective, the application of beliefs and learnings from this source opens up the infinite in obtaining whatever desires can be created, as long as they are for the highest good for all (see Appendix G, "Differences in Directing Your Life from the Mind [Logic] versus the Divine").

## LINKING THE MIND, THE BODY, AND THE DIVINE

We can now link Principles, Attitudes, and Practices to the illustration in Chapter Two that indicated how desired results can be organized into being, doing, and having. These are now linked to the Divine, the mind, and the body.

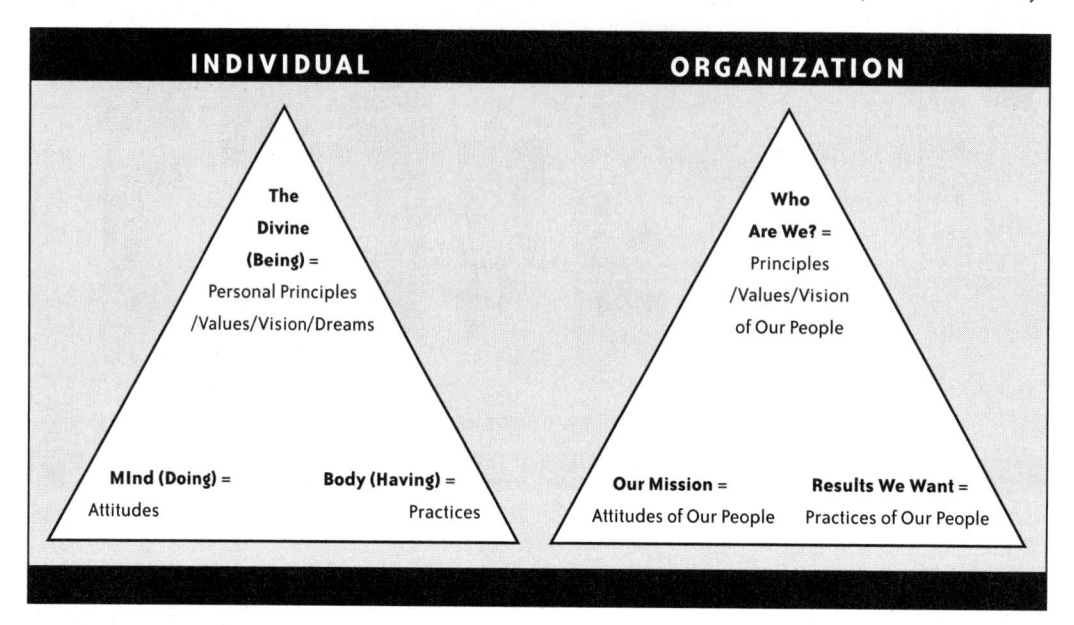

```
INDIVIDUAL                           ORGANIZATION

      The                                  Who
      Divine                               Are We? =
      (Being) =                            Principles
      Personal Principles                  /Values/Vision
      /Values/Vision/Dreams                of Our People


  Mind (Doing) =   Body (Having) =    Our Mission =        Results We Want =
  Attitudes        Practices          Attitudes of         Practices of
                                      Our People          Our People
```

Let's look at this linkage and bring it all together from an individual's viewpoint.

### INDIVIDUAL

The need to "become" all that you can be comes from the part of you that is the Divine. It is **fueled** by choosing *Principles* and *Values* from which your mind and body can function. This can be called your "ideal self." One of life's purposes is having the mind and body live in harmony with the Divine. This is having the full potential for experiencing Abraham Maslow's self-actualization.

The need to "do" all that you can comes from the mind, which is going all the time. The mind is always thinking. Being aware of your thoughts is the most powerful practice for getting desired results. It is **fueled** by choosing *Attitudes* that keep you open to having your Principles and values come through your thoughts. One of the greatest challenges of living, and being masters of our lives, is in making continuous efforts to bring the Divine and the mind in harmony and alignment with each other. Principles wither and die, losing their power, unless supported by Attitudes that keep the "garden hose" open and flowing with energy. Conversely, great Attitudes do not have a lot of power for being, doing, and having, if high standards and principles are not chosen. The results you can accomplish are infinite when you unite high ideals with great Attitudes.

The need to "have" (experience or enjoy) all that is possible comes from the body. Your body needs constant care and balance. Being aware of the emotions and feelings inside your body and properly managing them is another powerful practice. Your body is **fueled** by choosing *Practices* that keep the body open and moving forward. Principles and Attitudes create words and actions that lead to accomplishments.

The focus of your attention (Values and Principles through the Divine), creates thoughts (mind), that breeds feelings (body), that generates energy (the unseen force for achieving results), that motivates words and actions (body), that leads to desired results! They are all linked very closely together. High Principles, linked to positive Attitudes, connected to consistent Practices, generate the ability to achieve all that is possible in your life, and when brought together with others, in the life of all the organizations you are part of, it can be magnified many times over.

## APPLICATION EXAMPLE

One of the desired results could be to enjoy more success in your life, however you define success. But you may be held back by failures you have experienced that appear to be evidence of your inability to succeed.

**Principle:**
Belief that you are infinitely powerful in accomplishing all that you desire.

**Attitude:**
Failure is an illusion. Despite what the world says, you have not failed. You have had great learning experiences that have prepared you to be successful in whatever you choose. Stay with a positive focus in your life, no matter who or what shows up.

**Practice:**
Remain constantly aware of what your mind is thinking and what your body is feeling. When thoughts show up that do not support your belief (principle), immediately let them go and replace them with positive thoughts or a freedom

statement, reprogramming your mind to think in new ways towards success. When feelings of fear show up, take a moment to feel the emotion, then let it go. Keep your thoughts focused on the new paradigm/principle until feelings of confidence and success return.

As Principles, Attitudes, and Practices are continuously reviewed, all obstacles are overcome and the success you seek is realized. It may be difficult at first, but with persistence, it will get easier.

## ORGANIZATIONS

When your ability to consistently grow in these areas as an individual are united with others of like mind and heart, miracles are manifested through all the organizations you are part of. As your organization learns to align its Principles, Attitudes, and Practices with its members, great things will happen, and increased results will occur. Here are a few suggestions for any organization of any size, you are involved with:

1. Establish the organization's driving Principles and values, based on a clear and defined vision and mission statement (see Appendix L).
2. Be a model of the Attitudes that are wanted from the organization you are part of and for its people (customer service attitudes, etc.).
3. Determine which Practices are most important for the organization's people to be consistently practicing (be on time, accuracy, etc.).
4. Have the organization you are part of commit to being a learning and growing organization that embraces change, and constant self-renewal of the people and the organization.
5. Constantly adapt the Principles, Attitudes, and Practices based on the consistent review of what is being experienced that works.
6. Communicate clearly and in detail. Keep communicating and repeating. Make sure that there are constant conversations in meetings about "walking the talk." Keep the vision, mission, values, and goals in front of everyone's mind and talk about them all the time. Use the Personal Leadership guidelines suggested in Chapter Eight.
7. Be willing to risk and experiment. Learning will likely come before the actual desired results.
8. Do all that is possible to measure desired results. How will you know you are succeeding?
9. Keep people accountable, with love, acceptance, and support (see Chapter Twelve, "Realizing Your Full Potential and Freedom").

To continue the discussion of the linkage between Principles, Attitudes, and Practices, let's go back to the garden hose symbol.

*Principles* are the water (energy) that is stored behind the wall. An infinite supply of water can be generated when the highest Principles are chosen and applied.

*Attitudes* are the faucet that either turns the water on or off (or somewhere in between), depending on which Attitudes are adopted and how consistently they are applied.

*Practices* are the garden hose that brings forth the desired results.

These are all needed for the highest achievements possible. Selecting the appropriate ones for you and the organization you are part of, will bring results in alignment with those Principles, Attitudes, and Practices.

Chapters six through eleven suggest Principles, Attitudes, and Practices. The headings for each one describe the general results to be realized with their acceptance and application.

## PRINCIPLES

Principles are the fundamental laws or truths upon which a person's thoughts, words, and actions are based. It is the "come from" of an individual or organization, the core essence as reflected in all behavior, and a moral (either conduct or character from the point of right/wrong) standard. Because of the significance of being Principle-centered, note the words that *Roget's Thesaurus* gives of a Principle-centered person with high standards:

> Honest, upright, upstanding, virtuous, good, clean, honorable, full of integrity, reputable, credible, noble, sterling, manly, yeomanly, unimpeachable, blameless, unblemished, undefiled, pure, highly respectable, ethical, moral, high-minded, uncorrupted, true-hearted, true-dealing, law-abiding, fair, just, law-revering.

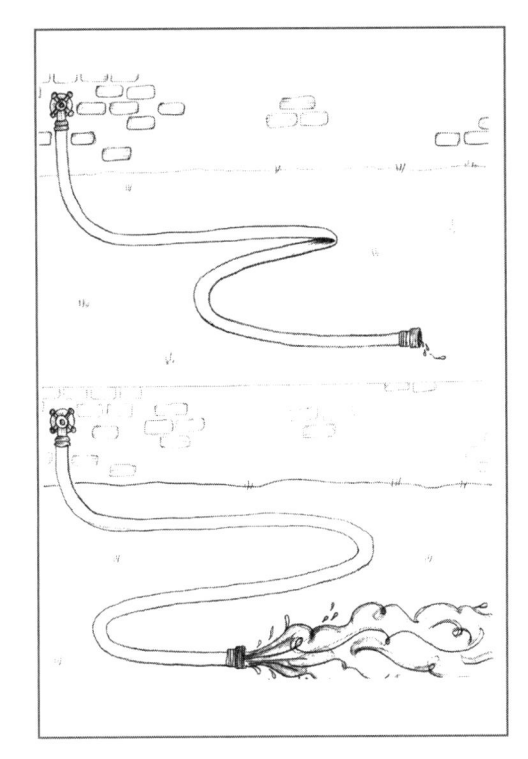

What a list! But this is exactly what the new millennium will draw out of us as more time goes on.

"It becomes obvious that if we want to make relatively minor changes in our lives, we can perhaps appropriately focus on our Attitudes and behaviors. But if we want to make significant, quantum change, we need to work on our basic paradigms." —STEPHEN R. COVEY

Principles are like gravity—they work no matter what. Principles become law and are at work in varying degrees in our lives, all the time. Regardless of circumstances, conditions, or events in the world around us, and the thoughts, feelings, or emotions in the world of our minds and bodies, they are the basis for what we choose as our behavior and the words we speak.

This does not mean that once Principles are in place we are perfect in living by them. (This is where they are not like gravity.) But it does mean they become our focus and we strive to live by them. To maximize their effectiveness, speak openly about Principles when appropriate. Our lives need to be a reflection of our chosen Principles—just like looking into a mirror is the reflection of our physical bodies.

When you read through the recommended Principles, think about them and feel whether they are appropriate for you. At the same time, remain open to the ones you choose to add or reemphasize. If you need to, find your own way to say them so they are true for you.

The suggested Principles, Attitudes, and Practices are shared as if you have chosen them and are able to constantly live by them. They are presented as if they were yours, rather than separate from you, and will serve you well as you examine if they are really who you are or chose to be.

**HERE ARE SOME SUGGESTIONS FOR HOW TO BE A PRINCIPLE-CENTERED PERSON:**

1. Be clear on which Principles are best for you. Only you can determine this, not any other outside source unless it is your Divine source. But choose! Proactively decide by what Principles you will strive to guide your daily thoughts, words, and actions. Assist the organizations you are involved with in all areas of your life to do the same.
2. Write them down and keep them physically close to you, so they are handy references to look at again and again.
3. Make them as detailed as necessary and be very clear what the word used (for example, the Principle "integrity") means to you. Have your mind and body be clear what the Principle means.

4. Continually play with them, evolve and even change them, as your life progresses and you get the results you seek. If you are not getting the results you seek, look again at the Principles directing your life.
5. Read them as often as possible until you know they are firm and steadfast in your memory, at least intellectually. (You are not being told how many times a day to do this or how long it will take. As a unique individual, only you can really decide on how many times and the length of time it will take. What you believe is likely the truth. But you will know, when one day you find yourself doing things differently based on the Principles you select or it becomes easier to have the Principle come up as a reminder of how to act and respond to life.)
6. Communicate your Principles to those you trust to support you, and won't judge when you are not speaking or acting from your Principles all of the time. "Support" means ways that you have communicated to them about how that looks to you. You are in control of what you want in life!
7. If you have a Divine source that you turn to, then ask for help in this effort.
8. Remain aware and conscious. Life will bring things to test you, and assist you to get what you desire. Life will also bring messages in various forms to assist you and help you to get even more clear. Stay mentally awake and aware!
9. Practice, Practice, Practice. Keep your mind focused on the Principles; immediately forgive yourself when you are not perfect; and keep going until the body automatically does what you have given clarity to with your selected Principles.
10. This one is vitally IMPORTANT! It ties into the concept presented in Chapter Ten, "Staying on a Roll." When you notice that you are acting as you have chosen to, then acknowledge it in a way that is appropriate for you. It could be just a conscious congratulations in your mind, gratitude in prayer, or something playful in celebration. You decide. Just make sure it is noticed and acknowledged. This part of the process will bring about the results you want faster. It will get easier the more you do this.

All of these steps are also appropriate and true for an organization.

## ATTITUDES

An Attitude is a mental position, opinion, or way of thinking that causes actions and reactions to life, all of which are reflected in the words, actions, thoughts, and behavior of an individual.

"The greatest discovery of my generation is that man can alter his life simply by altering his attitude of mind."  —WILLIAM JAMES

"The longer I live, the more I realize the impact of attitude on life. Attitude, to me, is more important than facts. It is more important than the past, than education, than money, than circumstances, than failures, than successes, than what other people think or say or do. It is more important than appearance, giftedness, or skill. It will make or break a company…a church…a home. The remarkable thing is we have a choice every day (every moment) regarding the attitude we will embrace for that day. We cannot change our past—we cannot change the fact that people will act in a certain way. We cannot change the inevitable. The only thing we can do is play on the one string we have, and that is our Attitude—I am convinced that life is 10 percent what happens to me and 90 percent how I react to it. And so it is with you—we are in charge of our attitudes."
—CHARLES SWINDOLL, *best-selling author, radio host, minister*

Attitude is a mental decision, affecting the physical body and its health and well-being. It can be a predetermined way you choose to look at and respond to life. Like the approach to Principle suggestions, the Attitudes in Chapters Six through Eleven are presented as if they are yours. You will decide which Attitudes are yours.

Let's go through a process that Enlightened Leadership International uses in experiencing the power of attitude for effective personal leadership.

What are the characteristics of a model leader?

1. _____  _____
2. _____  _____
3. _____  _____
4. _____  _____
5. _____  _____
6. _____  _____
7. _____  _____

Now go back through and decide whether the characteristic is an Attitude "A" or a Skill "S."

The following is a typical response by those participating in this process:

Characteristic Attitude/Skill

1. Deals with ambiguity. A
2. Trusting/Can be trusted. A
3. Receptive to ideas of others. A
4. Good listener. A/S
5. Actively looks for talents and skills of others. A/S
6. Fun. A
7. Leads themselves. A
8. Compassionate. A
9. Has a vision. A/S
10. Inspirational. A
11. Integrity. A
12. Respect. A
13. Communicates openly. A/S

From this list, 13 are Attitudes and four are also skills.

Attitude is what moves us forward in life. From your list, did you come to the same conclusion? Fortunately, *we* are the ones in charge of our attitudes. Attitude is a choice and we can change our attitude immediately. But we can't change someone else's attitude. The only person we can truly change is ourselves. However, it is a miracle to watch when one changes an attitude problem one has, how quickly it empowers others to follow. Our power to influence, to model change by example, is one of the great miracles of life.

Here is a true story that dramatizes the power of staying positively focused and always being at the point of choice with your attitude:

Jerry is a restaurant manager. He is always in a good mood and always has something positive to say. When someone would ask him how he was doing, he would reply, "If I were any better, I'd be twins!"

When he changed jobs, many of the waiters at his restaurant quit their jobs to follow him from restaurant to restaurant. The reason the waiters followed Jerry was because of his attitude. He was a natural motivator. If an employee was having a bad day, Jerry was always there, telling the employee how to look on the positive side of the situation.

One day Bill went up to Jerry and asked him, "I don't get it! No one can be a positive person all of the time. How do you do it?" Jerry replied, "Each morning I wake up and say to myself, I have two choices today. I can choose to be in a good mood or I can choose to be in a bad mood. I always choose to be in a good mood. Each time something bad happens, I can choose to be a victim or I can choose to learn from it. I always choose to learn from it. Every time someone comes to me complaining, I can choose to accept their complaining or I can point out the positive side of life. I always choose the positive side of life."

"But it's not always that easy," Bill protested. "Yes, it is," Jerry said. "Life is all about choices. When you cut away all the junk, every situation is a choice. You choose how you react to situation. You choose how people will affect your mood. You choose to be in a good mood or bad mood. It's your choice how you live your life."

Several years later, I heard that Jerry accidentally did something you are never supposed to do in the restaurant business: he left the back door of his restaurant open one morning and was robbed by three armed men. While trying to open the safe, his hand shook from nervousness and slipped off the combination. The robbers panicked and shot him. Luckily, Jerry was found quickly and rushed to the hospital.

After 18 hours of surgery and weeks of intensive care, Jerry was released from the hospital with bullet fragments still in his body. Bill saw Jerry about six months later. When I asked him how he was, he replied, "If I were any better, I'd be twins. Want to see my scars?" Bill declined to see his wounds, but did ask what had gone through his mind as the robbery took place.

"The first thing that went through my mind was that I should have locked the back door," Jerry replied. "After they shot me and I lay on the floor, I remembered that I had two choices: I could choose to live or I could choose to die. I chose to live." "Weren't you scared?" Bill asked. Jerry continued, "The paramedics were great. They kept telling me I was going to be fine. But when they wheeled me into the emergency room and I saw the expressions on the faces of the doctors and nurses, I got really scared. I read in their eyes, 'He's a dead man.' I knew I needed to take action."

"What did you do?" Bill asked. "Well, there was a nurse shouting questions at me," said Jerry. "She asked if I was allergic to anything. 'Yes,' I replied. The doctors and nurses stopped working as they waited for my reply. I took a deep breath and yelled, 'Bullets!' Over their laughter, I told them, 'I am choosing to live. Please operate on me as if I am alive, not dead.'"

Jerry lived thanks to the skill of his doctors, but also because of his amazing attitude. Bill learned from him that every day you have the choice to either enjoy your life or hate it. The only thing that is truly yours—that no one can control or take from you—is your attitude, so if you can take care of that, everything else in life becomes much easier. The results will naturally follow!

## PRACTICES

Practice is the pattern or habit of consistently doing something; to apply your beliefs and truths to your life until it is a desired habit, until the power (desired results) from the truth of the mind, is actually experienced in the body.

There are many Practices you will come up with that apply Principles and Attitudes that are able to get results more abundantly, easier ("flow state"), and quicker. This gives you greater freedom to serve people, and the organizations you are part of, more effectively.

### THE GARDEN HOSE: KINKING VERSUS FLOWING

| ▶ "Kinking the Garden Hose" (Desired results harder to achieve) | ▶ "Energy Flowing" (Desired results come easier, quicker, and more abundantly) |
|---|---|
| 1. Gets results from hard work through the mind and body. | 1. Unites body, mind, and spirit to get results. |
| 2. "I have limited capacity." | 2. "All things are possible." |
| 3. Attitude/choice: Evolutionary change. | 3. Attitude/choice: Revolutionary change. |
| 4. Read and learn. | 4. Read, learn, repeat, apply. |
| 5. No values/principles. | 5. Principle-centered. |
| 6. No clearly defined Attitudes drive my responses to life. | 6. Defined Attitudes practiced every moment. |
| 7. No practicing. | 7 Practices that bring results clearly defined and applied regularly. |

Add others that come up for you:
_____
_____
_____

Add others that come up for you:
_____
_____
_____

What has been of greatest value to you from reading this chapter?

_____
_____
_____

Is there something specific that you want to add to your desired results because of this value?

_____
_____

Is it worth power pausing now to complete a plan for the added result?
___ Yes ___ No

If yes, copy the Change Master Plan form (page 164) and create your future now.

_____
_____
_____

What will be your "I am" freedom statement to support your plan?

**Today, By Choice, I Am…**

_____
_____
_____
_____

# 6
# INDIVIDUAL AND ORGANIZATIONAL FREEDOM

## Principle: Choice

Individuals and organizations have the unique gift of choice. This gift carries with it the responsibility to use it wisely. It is a gift that operates very simply in our individual lives and our organizations. But because of this simplicity, it is possible to overlook its impact on our success and the ability to achieve desired results. This gift of choice naturally gives us a return in various forms, from what we have chosen. In this we can ask, what does choice mean?

Each choice we make, great and small, has a direct impact on the results we get. And those results may or may not be our desired results. This is why in Chapter Nine, the "Key to Freedom" principle is Integrity. We do what we say we're going to do, and our thoughts, words, and actions come from our chosen beliefs and principles.

On a personal level, an example could be as follows: You have decided to get your physical body back in good condition again. You have created a plan with five things you need to achieve this result. But as you go about your life, you consistently get distracted by the things that are in your world and the plan is never followed fully. You consistently fall back into the old patterns. The result you get is the same condition (or even worse) and the desired result gets lost.

Once we have selected the results we desire, our choices from moment to moment need to be in alignment with how we believe those results can be achieved. And if we do not get clear on what we want new, or more of, in our lives, then our choice, by default, has been to achieve nothing, or to get what the world brings us by chance. It means taking time when making these moment by moment choices and more thought given to the impact of the choices we are making.

Will you accept the direction of taking even greater responsibility for consistently being more? So you can get more of what you want in life, and so that you can give more to the organizations you are a part of? Your choice in answering these questions with what thoughts, feelings, words, and actions you bring forth, in each moment, can dramatically increase your true freedom in your life and your organizations, in accomplishing much more, sooner, and more joyfully as others join with you.

On an organizational level, it means taking extra time to consider the ramifications from the choices made from day to day. Does a new decision truly honor and value the people in the organization you are part of? Does each decision open up the opportunity to have your people grow and develop? Are decisions consistently out of balance in favor of profits? Is the mission statement more about what we want people to think about us, or is it about who we truly choose to be within the organization we are part of, and how we show up in the world we serve?

The possible answers to these questions are infinite. Think of your current relationship to the Principle of choice. Power pause and answer the question below, considering your life, and the life of each organization you are part of.

What are the choices you have made that are leading you toward the achievement of your desired results?

_____
_____
_____

As we go through the Principles and Attitudes in each chapter, there will be examples of a freedom statement. This can be developed as part of the vision we create for ourselves, and/or our organizations. Use it as a reference point to develop your own freedom statement, based on your own choices for your unique life.

> **CHOICE: FREEDOM STATEMENT POSSIBILITIES**
>
> **Individual** ↙     ↘ **Organization**
>
> "I am free to choose my life, and all that I am, all that I do, and all that I choose to have and enjoy. Whether my decisions are small ones made in the moment, or big ones affecting my whole life, I make those choices responsibly by considering their short and long-term impact on my life, the lives of others, and the results I am seeking. I ask, are they all in alignment? I choose to contribute my very best in every moment, without judgment or criticism to the organizations I am part of. I am committed to assisting these organizations to succeed. I choose to align myself with organizations that are consistent with my values."
>
> "The leadership in our organization chooses to be responsible for the directions we take by considering their short and long-term impact, not only on the success of the company, but equally on how it will affect the lives of our team members and associates. We have chosen our vision, mission, values, and goals based on who we are committed to be within the organization. We publish these not so much for the world to see, but for our own focus, for having impeccable integrity with what we say and what we actually do in practice from day to day."

If this is a Principle that serves you, power pause and develop your own freedom statement for your life. What are you willing to commit to with regard to being more responsible for the choices you make?

_____
_____
_____
_____
_____

## Attitude: Self-responsibility

Self-responsibility is an important Attitude that gives our choices in life more freedom of expression.

What does it feel like to you, when you see and hear someone taking full responsibility for what is in their life, rather than blaming someone or something else?

___

What impact do you experience in yourself or others in getting more and better results from life when "I am a victim" is replaced with "I am the only one responsible for what is in my life?"

___

Many people being responsible for their own lives generates more true freedom for individuals and organizations to get results reflecting the choices they have made. True empowerment (where much greater success is realized) is really self-empowerment, and comes from within, not from without. This is not to say that those who take the "victim" path are bad or wrong—some very dramatic and ugly things have been done to people which are outside their control and responsibility. (Appendix O, "Signs of Being a Victim," shares information about the victim mindset.) Hopefully those who do experience being a victim can be guided to some very capable people to assist them.

Self responsibility frees a "kinked garden hose"! It is one of the most dramatic attitudes that enlarge the "garden hose" for more energy to flow in creating success. If this Attitude is selected by you and your organizations, here are some suggested freedom statements to consider.

### SELF-RESPONSIBILITY: FREEDOM STATEMENT POSSIBILITIES

**Individual**

"I am the only one truly responsible for my thoughts, feelings/emotions, words, and actions. I blame no one, including myself, for the conditions and circumstances in my life. I proactively learn *and* apply things that come into my life, so that I am continually growing in my capacity to generate success personally, and in every organization I am part of. I accept personal responsibility for being and giving the best that I can in every moment and circumstance in my life."

**Organization**

"As an organization we are committed to assisting our associates in taking responsibility for their own lives, and what they contribute to our success. We are committed to hold ourselves responsible for our own success, and not blame outside circumstances for our lack of achievements. We create the environment that allows our people to contribute their ideas and suggestions freely, without judgment or criticism. We focus on empowering our people as much as possible, and encourage them to do their part in experiencing the true freedom of empowerment by each of them taking responsibility for their contributions."

## Attitude: Courage

"Life shrinks or expands in proportion to one's courage."
—ANAIS NIN

Sometimes we question our abilities to direct ourselves toward our accomplishments. What if I choose the wrong path? What if it doesn't work out? What if I lose everything? What if I fail? What if I am judged harshly by others? What if I'm alone?

At times, decisions are very difficult. Some people have a hard time making decisions with great confidence. But all decisions are right if they lead you to something that is good for all. Then you either get what you want (or more) or it will teach you something very important—leading you to what it is you do want. This is true as long as you are following what you feel is right. Life will gently guide you and make sure that you are okay. Ultimately, life will not give you something you cannot handle. Life makes this promise to all of us.

Courage is staying focused with positive focused questions that lead us forward. Take courage to go past previous limitations you have operated from on what you can accomplish. Take leaps of faith into new adventures knowing life will support you. Courage is breaking out in appropriate ways in each organization you are part of, in joining others for the good of the organization.

---

**COURAGE: FREEDOM STATEMENT POSSIBILITIES**

**Individual**

"I am a courageous person. I act upon what I feel are my next steps as I move forward in accomplishing all my goals and desires, no matter what problems or concerns come up. I courageously speak up with my input and insights in every organization I am a part of, for contributing to their success. If the emotion of fear ever comes up in my body, I observe it, and send it on its way by letting go and replacing it with confidence in who I am. My attitude is one of 'I can do it.' If I feel my body shrinking from something in the outside world, I simply stand up straight, take a deep breath, look forward with a positive outlook, and step forward with fresh courage as I pursue my life's endeavors."

**Organization**

"Our organization courageously remains open to the ways in which we can empower our associates, and help them empower themselves, in bringing more true freedom to them in succeeding in their jobs, while bringing more freedom to the company in reaching its desired results. We take calculated risks to our bottom line results in order to bring greater freedom and creativity to our people while allowing input from them that is heard, valued, and responded to."

---

## Practice: Practicing, Practicing, Every Day

Principles and Attitudes have little affect on generating the full potential of the results you and your organizations can achieve if the body is not speaking and acting from the same place. Having the body in alignment with your mind and the Divine within takes practice. For many people, it is their major purpose for being on the earth. It is no different than an Olympic champion and what he or she needs to do to get to the level of performance that brings the success they strive for.

The body cannot tell the difference between something vividly imagined and something actually experienced. Practicing can be done physically or mentally. Scientific research gives us evidence it will have the same effect.

The key to the effectiveness of using the imagination successfully is to bring into the pictured truth of the mind all the feelings that come into the body when what is desired is actually achieved. It is the "acting as if" concept discussed in Chapter Seven. It is important not to be distracted from the practice if at first the feelings don't come. They will as you persist. Also important in working with the imagination is to bring into play all the senses possible. See color; notice details of your desired result; and be committed to practice over and over throughout the day on those things you really choose to bring into your life.

> **PRACTICING: FREEDOM STATEMENT POSSIBILITY**
>
> "I know that true freedom in my life, and in the organizations I am part of, comes by choosing what is desired, then learning what it will take to achieve those results. Learning brings total freedom when I practice those steps that are necessary for realizing the results. I am like an Olympic athlete who knows practice (mentally and physically) each day is the only way to achieve success. I take all the things learned in my mind, and take the time to practice what I learn until I have experienced it, over and over again, in my body. I am then experiencing the feelings and results from greater freedom."

## Practice: Results Driven

This Practice is sometimes called creating your ideal vision, "beginning with the end in mind (Stephen R. Covey)," knowing the desires of your heart, intentional living, and goals.

It is paramount to be directed by clear desired results (the things you choose for your life), in detail, and *why* you want them. No matter what they are called, you will get what you are looking for/asking for, and more! But choose and be clear what it is that you want.

Organizations have a natural inclination to be results driven. Many have gone to great lengths to have vision and mission statements, and plans and goals on how to achieve them. It is vital to understand and communicate the "why" to what you have chosen. Desired results that do not generate good in the world will create unpredictable and inconsistent results, laden with ups and downs.

When a group of people is asked to achieve certain results, it's important to go deeper than just agreeing on results desired. If people are not aligned with the "what," the "how," *and* the "why," expected results will likely fall short. Normally, in a group setting *blame* is the focus, and an unhealthy atmosphere exists. However, this is not all bad! It is really an opportunity to stop (power pausing) and work together for understanding what the learnings are for each person involved. If the organization has, as one of its desires, to bring out the best in the organization and the people, then things will happen that will get everyone's attention. The original intent is not to have everything go perfectly. It is to get clear, be committed, learn, grow, adjust, and as a result of the process journey, "be" more of what will generate the desired results.

### Practice: Living from Passion

You will get the results you want faster and easier, and help your organizations get what they want faster and easier, if you are clear what it is that excites you in your life, and are actively involved in what that is for you. Ideally, what excites you is also what enables you to support you financially.

When you wake up in the morning, what excites you to have a new day in which to accomplish it?

*When the energy is harnessed from people living their life from their passion, the potential results are infinite!*

When organizations focus attention on hiring people whose passion can be linked with the needs of the organization, look to them to show "what is possible." One of the most powerful forces in life is seen when someone is living and working within those areas of their life they are the most excited about. An organization becomes much more powerful when it takes the time and is sincerely concerned about aligning people's passions with the vision, mission, and goals of the company.

There is enhanced freedom to achieve desired results when two or more people are aligned and passionate about something good for themselves, and the world. Living from your passion is one of the greatest ways to "enlarge the garden hose" for additional energy/momentum to achieve greater goals/results.

What are you passionate about?

_____
_____
_____

In their efforts to get bottom line results, organizations can accelerate their success by matching their needs with the passions of their people, and take the time, where possible, to discover what that passion is for each person.

If you are clear what it is that you live for, what generates great enthusiasm when you are doing it (or moving towards getting it), you can excel for yourself, and for the organizations you are part of.

> **LIVING FROM PASSION: FREEDOM STATEMENT POSSIBILITY**
>
> "I take time to pause my life and discover and rediscover what excites me. Everything that is in my life supports me in spending a substantial amount of my day enjoying what I love to do. I am living my life with great excitement because my passion in life is…"

## TRUE STORY

Steven was at one time a facilitator for a leadership training company. He loved the Principles he taught very much and enjoyed the opportunity to go out and share the program's tools and concepts. But he did not feel fulfilled. One day a company owner was having breakfast with Steven. A master at asking effective questions, the owner asked Steven if he could do anything he wanted to do, what would that look like. Steven said he would take the company's Principles to families and communities. The owner said, "Well, go for it." Steven did, and the rest is history and still going. Steven has developed a company that does just that. He has written two books published by Simon and Schuster, worked on several PBS television productions, and now travels all over the world serving people by delivering what he is passionate about—those family and community Principles that excite him. He is a true model of moving into passion, and getting more results for him personally, while serving the world more abundantly.

It is obviously unrealistic to think that everyone, in each organization, is going to go after his/her passion. That is not the point. But, for those who feel this untapped reservoir inside themselves looking for something that would really excite them, it would be well for them to pause and really get clear with it, and as is appropriate, move in that direction. Their "garden hose" would enlarge significantly by having the courage to go for it, like Steven.

Organizations who can match their needs within the organization with people's passion at what they do for the organization, have chosen to enlarge their "garden hose" for achieving greater results easier and quicker.

The only way to know this is true is by experiencing the difference passion makes in achieving more abundant dreams, goals, and desires. If you have not power paused to get in touch with your purpose/passion for being on the earth (thus having no central driving force in life), then you have chosen to be open to petty worries, fears, and whatever else life brings you.

Those organizations who have not taken some time to see how many people's passion they can tap into for the betterment of the organization, are missing a very big opportunity to substantially increase their power to achieve. It is a potentially risky move, and it takes time. Some people may leave in order to go some place that gives them the opportunity to live their passion. But the risk-reward ratio is very high! For passion is powerful in accomplishing more of the results you and organizations seek, and do it easier, faster, and much more joyfully.

Power pause and reflect on the things in this chapter that affect your ability to achieve desired results.

---

### THE GARDEN HOSE: KINKING VERSUS FLOWING

| ▶ "Kinking the Garden Hose" (Desired results harder to get) | ▶ "Energy Flowing" (Desired results come easier, quicker, and more abundantly) |
|---|---|
| 1. I am not in control of my life. | 1. I am totally free to choose. |
| 2. I work because I have to. | 2. I work in areas I am passionate about. |
| 3. I am not sure what I want in my life. | 3. I have clear goals. |
| 4. "Other people have made my life miserable." | 4. I am responsible for my life and I choose my freedom to be, do, and have whatever is for my best good. |
| 5. I learn constantly, but don't have time to practice it. Life is too fast paced. | 5. I take time to implement the important learnings I gain in my life. |

Add others that come up for you:

_____
_____
_____

Add others that come up for you:

_____
_____
_____

What has been of greatest value to you from reading this chapter?

_____
_____
_____

Is there something specific that you want to add to your desired results because of this value?

_____
_____
_____

Is it worth power pausing now to complete a plan for the added result?
___ Yes ___ No

If yes, copy the Change Master Plan form (page 164) and create your future now.

_____
_____
_____

What will be your "I am" freedom statement to support your plan?

**Today, By Choice, I Am…**

_____
_____
_____
_____

# 7
## THE POWER OF ONE

> "Men go abroad to wonder at the height of mountains, at the huge waves of the sea, at the long courses of the rivers, at the vast compass of the oceans, at the circular motion of the stars, and they pass by themselves without wondering." —SAINT AUGUSTINE

The single greatest learning in life for an individual is to remember and experience who they really are. This adventure in self-discovery will ultimately lead others to remember that same infinite greatness within themselves.

There is so much untapped power (experts say limitless) in us. As we value and honor each other, supporting each other in the process of change and growth, our power to *be, do,* and *have* dramatically increases. As we unite with others who choose to tap into their own power, for any cause for good, we all will experience the freedom to achieve desired results to a much greater degree. This is the essence of the change and the evolution of the human race through life's conditions, circumstances, and events, and within people themselves in the new millennium.

Before reviewing the suggested Principle, Attitude, and Practices for believing in who you are and what you can achieve, here is some introductory information as reminders of things you may have heard or read about many times. Repetition is a good thing.

### Who Are We?

For each one of us, who we are depends directly on ourselves. What are you willing to allow yourself to achieve in the three areas of *being, doing,* and *having* or enjoying? Answering this question also gives any organization a glimpse of what it can achieve.

*Any organization is only as good as its people—each one of them!*

Our power to grow by choice from the inside out, or to grow as change is thrust on us from the outside in, depends on the limitations or infinite possibilities we place on ourselves. From nature comes a powerful example:

In the Grand Canyon in Arizona, there is an old juniper tree. The twisted and gnarled tree had grown from the side of a rock canyon wall. To look at it you wondered how such a tree could grow from solid rock. To know its history is to learn a fascinating truth about life.

A juniper seed fell into a crevice near the edge of the canyon wall. Everything was solid rock. With the crevice having no soil, little water, and no sunlight, it would seem impossible to have this seed grow into a tree. But the seed knew no limitations. It germinated. It established roots. It grew. Eventually a shoot raised up through the crevice where it found sunshine and water from rain. As it grew, the roots began to exert pressure on the outer ledge of the rock. The pressure grew, eventually becoming so great that one section of the canyon wall broke loose and crumbled; forty million tons of rock fell one mile down to the base of the canyon. The tree never gave up, and never recognized any limitations. Its power was tremendous, providing us with a dramatic truth about our lives.

"The potential for the human race is almost infinite."
—DR. RICHARD LEAKEY

"Once people get over preconceived ideas about limitations, they can be much more."   —WILLIAM JAMES

## Freedom through "Resetting the Zero"

One of the most powerful tools Enlightened Leadership International teaches is what they call "Resetting the Zero." In terms of getting results more abundantly, easier, and quicker, it is an important concept to understand. This concept can dramatically effect self-esteem, a key factor for life achievement.

List three characteristics that are your greatest strengths, and three you feel are your greatest weaknesses. After listing them, rate them from a –5 up to a +5 with an "X." As you go through this exercise, it will be more powerful if you are aware of how your body is feeling.

### THREE GREATEST STRENGTHS

-5 +5 _____   -5 -3 0 3 +5

-5 +5 _____   -5 -3 0 3 +5

-5 +5 _____   -5 -3 0 3 +5

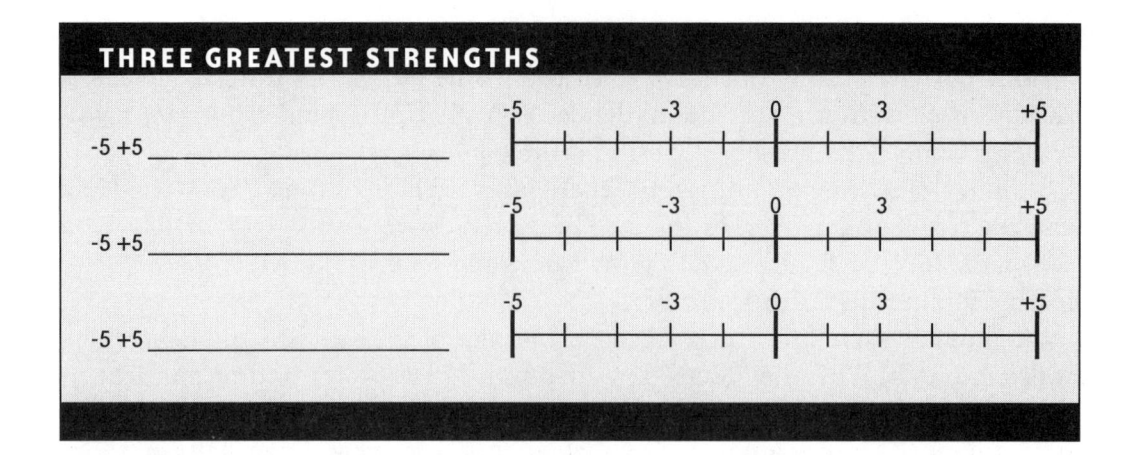

### THREE GREATEST WEAKNESSES

-5 +5 _____   -5 -3 0 3 +5

-5 +5 _____   -5 -3 0 3 +5

-5 +5 _____   -5 -3 0 3 +5

The intent of this exercise is to have you experience a major shift in your power to move forward more successfully with your desired results. You may also discover how you have been deceived in the past. Ed Oakley, CEO of Enlightened Leadership International, calls it "the ultimate deception." This "deception" has a direct impact on your life and the way you relate to others, and those in your organizations. It may be a very deep seeded belief you have about yourself. If this is true, you can experience the application of a new truth called "the ultimate self-empowerment tool."

Answer the following question before reading on:

How do you measure darkness?

_____
_____

Since there are only light meters, not darkness meters, the only way to answer this question is to put it in terms of the degree of light that can be measured. The answer is darkness is measured by some degree of light, all the way down to zero light.

Let's try this again on another topic:
How do you measure cold?

_____
_____
_____

We are only able to measure the degree of heat above absolute zero. Like darkness, cold is measured by some degree of heat, down to zero.

The next question must seem obvious:
How do you measure weakness?

_____
_____
_____

The answer to this question leads us to the new "ultimate self-empowerment tool." You only have strengths! We have no weaknesses, only strengths, measured again from zero. There is not a single person on the planet that has less than no strength.

This is not just a play on words, or simply a positive mental attitude in disguise. There is power in this concept.

How does it feel to have no weaknesses? Does it sound untruthful?

_____
_____
_____

CHAPTER SEVEN: THE POWER OF ONE

List below the six characteristics you listed previously and rate them. But this time, change the –5 to zero, the zero to +5, and the +5 to +10 (thus the term "resetting the zero" was created). Use the same rating you did before, but now, for example, a –3 is a +2.

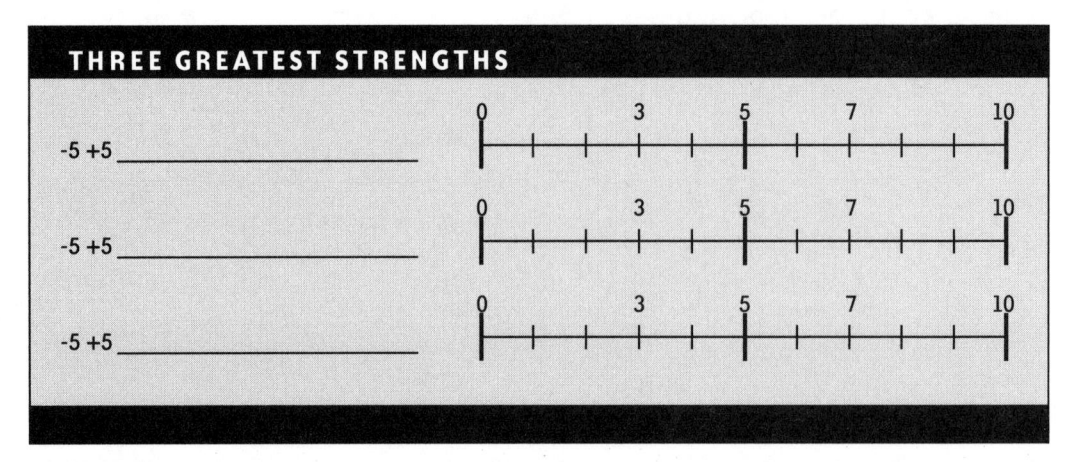

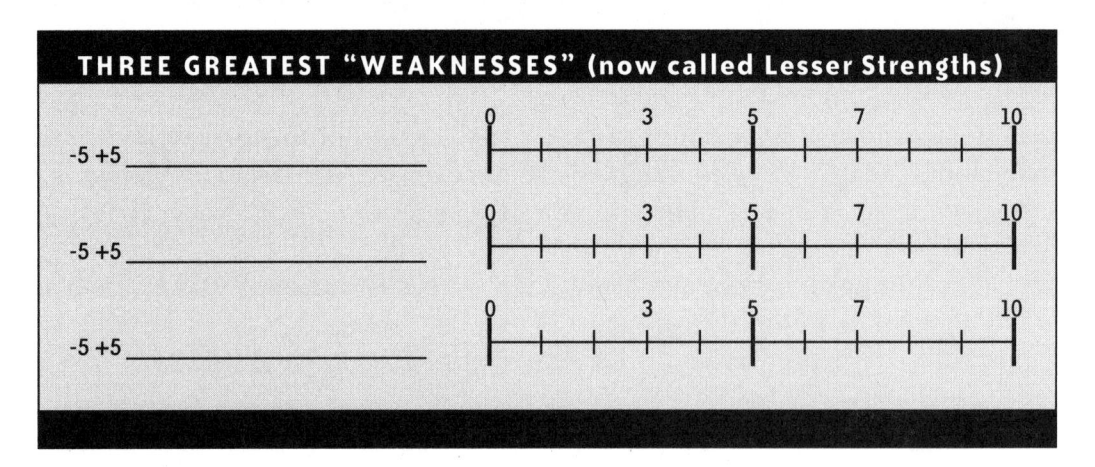

### THREE GREATEST STRENGTHS

-5 +5 _____  0 —— 3 —— 5 —— 7 —— 10

-5 +5 _____  0 —— 3 —— 5 —— 7 —— 10

-5 +5 _____  0 —— 3 —— 5 —— 7 —— 10

### THREE GREATEST "WEAKNESSES" (now called Lesser Strengths)

-5 +5 _____  0 —— 3 —— 5 —— 7 —— 10

-5 +5 _____  0 —— 3 —— 5 —— 7 —— 10

-5 +5 _____  0 —— 3 —— 5 —— 7 —— 10

What feelings/emotions did your body experience when you went from being a minus number to a positive number? And from a small positive number to a larger one?

_____
_____
_____

How important is this concept to you? What meaning can this have for you?

_____
_____
_____

To help you understand even more and experience the importance of the concept that there only degrees of strength with every one of your characteristics, here is another analogy.

Assume that we want to increase the temperature of the small block of ice on the left, and the pan of water on the right, both by four degrees. Which one will take the most heat to accomplish?

It is the block of ice, because you have to change the current state of the water from ice to liquid which takes about 80 times more energy. It would take 80 times the energy to go from a weakness to a strength, and far less energy to go from a +3 to a +5 in your characteristics.

Using the concept of the garden hose, when we see weakness in ourselves, we "kink the garden hose" to some degree and results come with greater difficulty. When we look at ourselves as having degrees of strength, we are keeping the "garden hose" more open, and more free in having the energy to achieve.

-2 C to +2 C     +1 C to +5 C

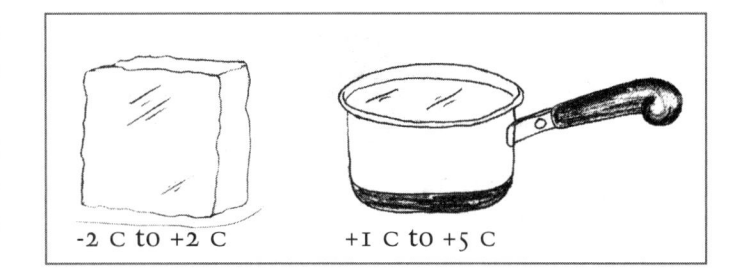

"Shifting the zero" can create a very real positive emotional response. Here is a personal application story: I remember well when I first experienced the effects of this powerful shift. By the way, I learned about this concept intellectually over two years before this actual experience. The real impact on my life for experiencing my growth was minimal until this experience with the truth occurred. Three manila folders were placed on the ground about five feet apart. The first one was marked "-5," the second was marked "0," and the third "+5." I was in a group of about six people. We were asked to take one of our weaknesses and stand where we had judged ourselves to be. I remember being a -3 with one of the weaknesses I had identified. They asked us to feel what that was like, that is, to be a -3. Then they turned the folders over and replacing the -5 was 0, and the 0 was +5, and the +5 was turned into a +10. Therefore I was a +2 with my so-called weakness. I remember my body feeling a definite emotional shift, a shift that gave me more energy. I thought and felt better about myself, and I wanted to increase the strength (rather than overcome a weakness) of what I had termed a weakness. I had more energy by far, to move forward more successfully. It was more than a positive mental attitude change. It was feeling, or emotional shift, which was the real source of new energy, which of course came from a mental change in attitude. "I have no weaknesses. I only have various degrees of strength." This is real energy (to accomplish more) going from a "kinked" state to more of a "flow" state.

What was your experience with this exercise?

_____
_____
_____

If we see weakness in others, we "kink" the ability in our relationships, and all of our organizations, to get desired results. Life just simply works this way. It is "the ultimate deception." When we "shift the zero," it is the ultimate self-empowerment tool. When this leadership quality is being further developed in us, it is also a perfect way to empower others. Your focus and experience with this concept can prove it for yourself. The effort is well worth it if you seek to achieve greater success in your life, and in the lives of others in each organization you are part of.

> "Our deepest fear is not that we are inadequate—Our deepest fear is that we are powerful beyond measure. It is our light, not our darkness that most frightens us.
>
> "We ask ourselves, who am I to be brilliant, gorgeous, talented and fabulous? Actually who are you not to be? You are a child of God. Your playing small doesn't serve the world. There is nothing enlightened about shrinking so that other people won't feel insecure around you. We were born to make manifest the glory of God within us. It is not just in some of us; it is in everyone.
>
> "And, as we let our own light shine, we unconsciously give other people permission to do the same. As we are liberated from our own fear, our presence automatically liberates others."
>
> —MARIANNE WILLIAMSON, *A Return to Love*

## Principle: Belief in Who We Are

> **BELIEF IN WHO WE ARE: FREEDOM STATEMENT POSSIBILITY**
>
> "I believe in myself and my power to accomplish all I choose for my life. I contribute my best to all who are in my life. I believe I have infinite capacities, mentally, physically, and spiritually, and do not limit my potential. I believe I can be, do, and have what I am free to choose. I believe I am of infinite worth to the world around me. My words and actions support this belief, and I confidently take action on my choices, knowing that I will succeed. If fear and doubt show up, I hold on to this belief until those false emotions are gone. I have a very clear vision for myself, and each day I am realizing more of its fulfillment."

"In order to succeed we must first believe we can."
—MICHAEL KORDA

"What great thing would you attempt if you knew you could not fail?"
—ROBERT SCHULLER

If you really believe it, then your actions will more and more support that belief and you will take action confidently. If fear shows up, seeing and feeling your belief will see you through it. Pause and become more aware of what you believe in, and what you can achieve, after reading the following story:

Fifteen of the greatest scientists in the world met in the United States. Their job was to do one thing: determine the ultimate in physical effort that a human being can give. They had all the money, time, and facilities they needed.

But what was the ultimate? How high could a man jump, no matter what kind of shape he was in, how long he took, or how many years went by? What was the ultimate he could ever jump?

So they set a mark—this was the ultimate. Man would never go over the mark, even if two thousand years went by—he would never go over this mark. It was physiologically impossible. They did this in fifty areas. The marks were way above what people were doing at the time.

*Fifteen years later, every mark in all fifty areas was broken—some by 15 and 16 year olds.*

Here is even more evidence for keeping an open mind about limitations:

"I think there is a world market for maybe five computers."
—THOMAS WATSON, *Chairman of IBM, 1943*

"There is no reason anyone would want a computer in their home."
—KEN OLSON, *President, Chairman, and Founder of Digital Equipment Corporation, 1977*

"I have traveled the length and breadth of this country and talked with the best people, and I can assure you that data processing is a fad that won't last out the year."
—*Editor in charge of business books for Prentice Hall, 1957*

"This 'telephone' has too many shortcomings to be seriously considered as a means of communication. The device is inherently of no value to us."
—*Western Union internal memo, 1876*

"A cookie store is a bad idea. Besides, the market research reports say America likes crispy cookies, not soft and chewy cookies like you make."
—*Response to Debbi Fields' idea of starting Mrs. Field's Cookies*

"We don't like their sound, and guitar music is on the way out."
—DECCA RECORDING COMPANY, *rejecting the Beatles, 1962*

"I'm just glad it'll be Clark Gable who's falling on his face and not Gary Cooper."   —GARY COOPER *on his decision not to take the leading role in Gone With the Wind*

"So we went to Atari and said, 'Hey, we've got this amazing thing, even built with some of your parts, and what do you think about funding us? Or we'll give it to you. We just want to do it. Pay our salary, we'll come work for you.' And they said, 'No.' So then we went to Hewlett-Packard, who said, 'Hey, we don't need you. You haven't got through college yet.'"
—STEVE JOBS, *Founder of Apple Computer, on attempts to get Atari and HP interested in his and Steve Wozniak's personal computer.*

"Computers in the future may weigh no more than 1.5 tons."
—*Popular Mechanics, forecasting the relentless march of science, 1949*

"The concept is interesting and well-formed, but in order to earn better than a 'C', the idea must be feasible."   —*A Yale University management professor in response to Fred Smith's paper proposing reliable overnight delivery service (Smith went on to found Federal Express).*

"Airplanes are interesting toys but of no military value."
—MARECHAL FERDINAND FOCH, *Professor of Strategy, Ecole Superieure de Guerre*

Pause and reflect on this infinite possibility question: What great thing(s) would you attempt if you knew you could not fail?

_____
_____
_____
_____
_____

CHAPTER SEVEN: THE POWER OF ONE

## Attitude: All Things Are Possible

### ALL THINGS ARE POSSIBLE: FREEDOM STATEMENT POSSIBILITIES

**Individual**

"I am unlimited in my abilities to get the results I choose in my life. I am infinite in my abilities to help the organizations I am with. As I reflect on what I want to be in my life, what I want to be doing, and what I want to have, I am open to all possibilities so that my very best can come forward in my life. I freely and openly spread this Attitude to others I am with. Because I am experiencing more of the results I have chosen, this Attitude is more than simply a "positive mental attitude." I am experiencing more true freedom in my life."

**Organization**

"Our vision has aspects to it that seem impossible. But our team members share a common belief in our ability to work as a team and accomplish whatever we choose as desired results. When obstacles appear, we come together and solve them. We see obstacles as opportunities to work together to solve the challenges confronting us. We maintain the attitude that all the answers to all our questions, and all the solutions to all our challenges are within the people in our organization. All team members are valued, because we know that at any given time, someone new comes forth with a key answer or solution. We are a team who values each other, knowing that not any one person has all the answers all of the time."

It is an exciting thing to watch people and organizations reach for much more than they have ever attempted before. It has two very significant benefits:
1. More of what you really want is achieved and enjoyed, and
2. More learnings are gained along the way.

As those learnings are taken into your experience, true freedom (power) to achieve more is possible.

This can be made even more clear by the experience of diamond miners in South Africa. At first, people found a few diamonds in the yellow clay, and were delighted with their good fortune. They supposed this would be the full extent of their find. However, in digging deeper, they came upon blue clay. To their amazement, they found as many precious stones in a day as they had previously found in a year. What seemed like wealth faded into insignificance beside the new riches.

Take the risk of reaching for all that you can possibly dream (blue clay) of achieving as an individual or as an organization, and not be satisfied with mediocrity (yellow clay). If you can believe that all things are possible, then the only limitation is your own unwillingness to dream and create.

## Practice: Being Aware

"Awareness is the source of joy."   —RICHARD EYRE

"Achievement is the inevitable and natural by-product of awareness."
—TIMOTHY GALLWAY

The answers, solutions, and directions a person receives for his/her life are directly related to the questions she/he are running on. Awareness is the bridge between the two. When we ask questions for our lives, for others, or for our organizations, waiting and watching for the answers to come creates the need for us to be aware of what is going on internally and externally. For the answers in life will come, but how they come really varies.

I have found some answers in the brevity of bumper stickers and license plates. At one point in my life, I felt a mental and emotional bondage and unable to make my own decisions. I sought freedom in my own unique way. Soon after that I came upon a license plate that I had obviously never seen before. It read "UR FREE." It helped to change my attitude which affected my thoughts, words, and actions. True freedom began to follow, and has grown since then.

Getting into the habit of being aware of your thoughts, feelings, emotions, words spoken, actions, and "life's messages" from the outside world we all share, is a powerful key to helping us realize more of our desired achievements in life. It helps us be self-responsible for our lives. It takes constant focus to be aware and conscious of our lives as they progress. You will be amazed, if not already, at how much you react unconsciously. You were not born this way, but the unconscious strengthens itself as the stresses and responsibilities of life crash down. The next Practice contains information about leading from within, which will strengthen your understanding of this Principle to see if it is one you want to incorporate/increase.

This very powerful practice can also assist an organization, in the same way it serves an individual. However, there is the additional powerful benefit of having more than an individual involved in being aware, if the organization supports such a philosophy. It may feel like a risk to the managers within an organization, but with controls and guidelines, it is a very powerful opportunity for an organization to realize success not thought possible.

## Practice: Leading from Within

A Rutgers University study of Fortune 500 CEOs found the thing they had in common is that they relied heavily on their intuition and the intuition of their people. By balancing intuition with traditional approaches, individuals and organizations can move very quickly in getting more results, more easily, and faster. It can make it an exciting, rejuvenating time to be alive!

Intuition uses the power of pausing, quieting the mind and body, and taps into the source of the Divine for immediately knowing something without the conscious use of reasoning. This is done through asking positive focused questions that begin with how, possibly what, but never WHY.

This Practice is one of the greatest aids in the process of flowing with the inevitable changes that occur. It continues to be important to look within ourselves and inquire to find answers and understanding about our lives, and the life of our organizations.

What is really exciting is that through this "process," we find ourselves naturally maturing and growing into higher levels of successful character *and* performance!

In Appendix F you will find "Twelve Habits for Leading from Within (Intuition)." Take time to look this over. What is the greatest value you receive from what she suggests?

_____
_____
_____

What would be of highest value for you to add or to change to fit your particular beliefs?

_____
_____
_____

Suggestions for beginning/enhancing your practice to lead from within:
1. Believe that a Divine source exists and that it has all the answers.
2. Slow down...and consistently stop!
3. Consistently ask questions that are important to you for successfully guiding your life and the lives of the organizations you are part of.
4. Listen for answers.
5. Be willing to learn new things.
6. Courageously act upon direction received.
7. Be thankful.
8. Keep a journal and share your successes.
9. Freedom statements and affirmations.
10. Service to others, the organizations you are part of, and to all life.
11. Be a good person.
12. Develop your intuition with others.

As a final thought, look at Appendix G, "Differences in Directing Your Life from the Mind (Logic) versus the Divine" to compare the logical approach to directing your life, versus going with the Divine.

How do you know you are getting information from human life or the Divine, and so are leading from within? Anita Cameron, President of Business Success Made Simple, has developed some excellent material for this highly simple, and yet complicated subject. The complication comes from people, not the way the Divine works!

She titles her work in this area "Decisions Made Simple." She suggests some ways to determine whether the Divine is being tapped for desired direction:
- The Divine leads to good for everyone involved.
- It is never in a hurry, and never late.
- It operates now, in the present, not in the past or the future.
- Only truth comes forth without confusion.
- Other indications are:
    Peace accompanies such direction.
    There is only love, no judgments.

There is not an indication of right or wrong, or good or bad.
> It just is.

You will feel expansion, an openness, with ideas flowing gently.
- When the Divine is involved in the process, results include:
  More consistent right decisions/answers that lead more quickly, and with less effort, to the desired results.
  Higher self-esteem.
  Confidence.
- The process becomes fun and adventurous.
  More productivity and bottom line results with less doing.
  Enthusiasm and excitement for life.
  Creativity and innovation.

As a final thought, look at Appendix G, "Differences in Directing Your Life from the Mind (logic) versus the Divine," comparing the logical approach to directing your life, versus going to the Divine.

What has been your greatest value from this information?

_____
_____
_____

Along the way as we develop from our birth, who we really are often fades, and much of our full potential goes with it. For achieving all our desires, our success can be accelerated by living by the compass (the Divine), not the clock (the world). Here is what one expert says about genius percentages at various ages:

### GENIUS PERCENTAGES AT VARIOUS AGES

| | |
|---|---|
| From three to five years old | 100% |
| From five to 10 it drops to | 32% |
| From 10 to 15 it drops to | 23% |
| From 15 to 20 it drops to | 10% |
| Older than 20 years old it drops to | 2% |

—From *Creativity in Business* by Michael Ray

### LEADING FROM WITHIN: FREEDOM STATEMENT POSSIBILITIES

**Individual**

"I am a person who receives Divine direction in all areas of my life, for my benefit and the benefit of all my organizations. I pause as needed, quiet my mind, and ask questions in areas that need attention. I believe that all the answers I need for my success are within me, and I trust the answers that come forth. As a result of this practice, I achieve more of my desired results faster and easier, and with less effort on my part."

**Organization**

"We believe in the people who make up our organization. We empower them by encouraging them that when tough issues arise, or when direction is needed for them to perform their job, that they get quiet, ask specific questions, and go within to seek guidance. We have established organizational boundaries along with this empowerment so that for minor decisions they are empowered to be on their own if they choose. But if the direction needed has a significant impact on others or the organization, others need to be involved to confirm the chosen direction."

There are not many organizations that allow this practice, but the trend is definitely growing, and growing rapidly. Organizational boundaries are needed in detail, well communicated, and a planned follow-up program. As organizations take the risk with this practice, they are enlarging that "garden hose" significantly. The infinite source of Divine energy is more available to support us getting what we desire. Rather than simply relying on human power, with all its limitations, there now can be an ability to tap into an infinite power. But again, well thought out and communicated boundaries need to be established with accountability.

## Practice: Acting As If

Experience has shown that we will get the results we choose sooner and easier if we act as if they are already accomplished. If you want to be more patient, be as clear as you can what the result looks and feels like, and immediately act as if it was done. When impatience shows up, briefly acknowledge it (stuffing, or ignoring, or judging it as wrong/bad has proven not to work—it slows the progress) and let it go like a butterfly off your shoulder into the breeze, and not judge yourself for not measuring up to your new ideal. Simply stay focused (remember: you get more of what you focus on) on being patient. It will be a part of your life much sooner.

The great seventeenth century French general Vicomte de Turenne was known for marching into battle at the head of his troops. Asked about it, he replied, "I conduct myself like a brave man, but all the time I'm afraid. I don't give in to the fear, but say to my body, 'Tremble, old carcass, but walk!' And my body walks!"

Since feelings are the real power (or energy) for getting the results we want in our life, it is important to remember that when we mentally "act as if" with something new we desire, often the feelings are just not there. When this happens, simply persist and the feelings of accomplishing what is being created will come, and the actual results will certainly follow. Remain diligent and persist.

Pause and determine what value this practice of "acting as if" has for you:

_____
_____
_____

## Shared Leadership

Regardless of position or title, everyone is a leader, with potential contributions to make toward the success of their organizations. This leads to the concept of shared leadership, where organizations look to each person for what they can contribute. When they listen, value, and act upon appropriate suggestions, the momentum increases, the culture becomes more open, and more results are achieved more quickly and easily.

Research has shown that when in this flight pattern, geese fly 72 percent faster than when one goose flies alone. The lead goose breaks the wind and sets the air in motion, then the rest of the flock follow in the wake. When the lead goose tires, it drops toward the back and another goose takes over.

If everyone chooses to participate, Personal Leadership is a responsibility shared by everyone. We are all leaders, and are charged with coming forth with our very best when it is needed and appropriate.

In Canada, large draft horses are put to a weight pulling contest each year. One year, a horse was able to pull 9,000 pounds and the number two horse was able to pull 8,000 pounds, or a combined weight of 17,000 pounds. A test was arranged to see what would happen if both horses pulled together. They pulled the 17,000 pounds. Then weights were loaded until the horses pulled a combined total of 32,000 pounds, proving the power of uniting to work together towards a common goal. Two horses together could pull more than their combined individual weight.

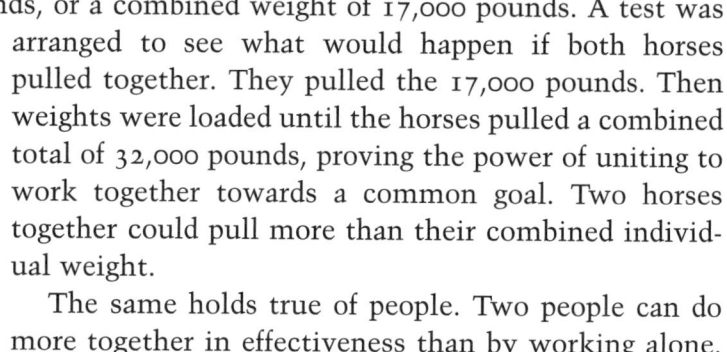

The same holds true of people. Two people can do more together in effectiveness than by working alone. This is the power of united and aligned teams.

The answers are all within the people in your organization. This does not mean you don't go outside for help, but within the organization's people are the answers. Solutions that possibly are received through people from the outside, will likely come from contacts within.

Organizations need to create a safe environment for leadership to be given by all—this is the ideal. How? People will generally contribute freely if they know they will not be judged for their opinions, and definitely if they know that their jobs will not be on the line for speaking up. People need to feel safe. The organization's positive, non-judgmental reactions to opinions and suggestions is vital to creating a trusting environment, filled with openness and leadership that truly listens and values everyone's ideas. If this environment does not now exist, a very deep commitment to it, in words and actions that support the commitment, patience, and time, all is needed to allow it to grow. Many companies have incentive programs for new ideas. I have found that the greatest success comes from empowering people from within themselves, and encouraging this atmosphere—it is more effective than external stimulants.

## Teams Working Effectively Together

When you look at the potential of people working together for a common good, the potential power for getting desired results remains untapped. The potential to accomplish the impossible is so real, that it is worth all of our efforts to continually strive to find all the keys to make consistently tapping into this potential possible. Here are some reminders:

- A deep and sincere valuing, honoring, and love (caring) for the people that you associate with, dedicating yourself to helping them get what they want in their lives, as they help you and the organization do the same.
- A high awareness and commitment about the infinite energy, or life force, that is available to us, and what "kinks the garden hose" at any given moment and what keeps the water (energy) flowing smoothly and easily, with a commitment to keep learning how all this works and apply what is learned from day to day.
- Living from the Principle that synergy is real (1 + 1 = 3 or more, and can be much more), and from the attitude that you will dedicate yourself, and help others to do the same, in doing whatever it takes to tap into this unlimited potential. Embrace the practice of being willing to get into teams with a common purpose and make them a laboratory of learning, growing, and achieving desired results together.
- A personal commitment to bring out more of the very best within yourself, with an openness to change from *already being good* to *getting better*. Here are some of the ways to help bring this about:
    - Use the Personal Leadership guidelines in Chapter Eight for keeping the energy positive and creative in meetings.
    - Frequent individual and collective power pausing to keep the process of renewal and change at a very high level.
    - Knowing from experience that the answers to all the questions and solutions to all the challenges organizations face, can come from the teams within the organization, especially when those teams are committed to applying the power of the Divine within them to assist their efforts. In addition, let freedom-based questions direct the attention of the group.
    - Support free and open discussions without judgment or criticism,

while maintaining a positive-focused, solution-oriented approach to what needs to be discussed.

Very clear, concise, frequent, repetitive communications with the intent of keeping everyone informed and allowing for the flow of constant feedback. Feedback is the breakfast of champions!

An awareness of how emotions work in a team setting and have an organized, well thought out plan to deal with them as they come up. This includes a unified commitment and permission from all to do that, for the sake of learning, growing, and working together for achieving exciting results.

Keep your stewardship and accountability Principles well in place, if appropriate, for all who are on the team. These Principles are not for control and manipulation with judgment, but for clarifying responsibilities with love, acceptance, and support.

Find balance between actual solutions, directions, and answers and the fact that the issues being faced in the meeting have at their deepest levels, the intent to help people work together more effectively. This may feel risky, but when the greater results come more easily and faster, the tangible evidence will support

---

### THE GARDEN HOSE: KINKING VERSUS FLOWING

| ▶ "Kinking the Garden Hose" (Desired results harder to get) | ▶ "Energy Flowing" (Desired results come easier, quicker, and more abundantly) |
|---|---|
| 1. I'm not capable. | 1. I believe in myself. |
| 2. I work hard for what I have. | 2. I unite in balance body, mind, and the Divine in accomplishing all that I desire. |
| 3. I have weakness. | 3. I only have strengths. |
| 4. I can't do that. | 4. All things are possible. |
| 5. My thoughts ramble all the time. | 5. I am consciously aware of what's going on in and around me. |

Add others that come up for you:

_____

_____

Add others that come up for you:

_____

_____

more balance. Momentum will build quickly and enthusiastically with this kind of open and learning environment.

What has been of greatest value to you from reading this chapter?

_____
_____
_____

Is there something specific that you want to add to your desired results because of this value?

_____
_____
_____

Is it worth power pausing now to complete a plan for the added result?
___ Yes ___ No

If yes, copy the Change Master Plan form (page 164) and create your future now.

_____
_____
_____

What will be your "I am" freedom statement to support your plan?

**Today, By Choice, I Am…**

_____
_____
_____
_____

CHAPTER SEVEN: THE POWER OF ONE

# 8
## FREEDOM TO THRIVE ON CHANGE

"Maintaining the status quo is more dangerous than launching into the unknown." —ANONYMOUS

Many of us spend significant parts of our lives stuck in thought and behavior patterns that keep us at a standstill, or with minimal "newness of life." This can also be true for our organizations. What creates change is what life brings us, and forces us to change. This chapter is about being more proactive with what is in our lives, and being guided by our beliefs, dreams, and desires.

In the following chart, there are things that indicate if you are maintaining or creating life. Put a check mark next to all the ones that apply to you and add ones not on the list. The final chart will be the list from which you can give new direction to your life.

## MAINTAINING VERSUS CREATING

▶ **Maintaining**
**("kinked garden hose")**
**When not balanced with creating**

No defined vision, goals.
Not excited about life.
Outside world is generating most of your change.
Patterns/habits direct each day's activities.

No balance.
Resisting change.
Not much learning.
Not applying what little is learned.

No new creations in any area of your life.
Change is forced on you.

Add your own observations:
_____
_____
_____

▶ **Creating ("flow state")**
**When balanced with maintaining**

Clear vision and goals.
Living in passion.
Inner world (being proactive by choice) creates the changes you experience.
Create new things in each day along with what has to be done.

Balanced in all areas of life.
Accept change.
Learning.
Enthusiastically applying what key things are learned.

Always creating new things.
Change is generated proactively based on desired results.

Add your own observations:
_____
_____
_____

CHAPTER EIGHT: THRIVE ON CHANGE

## Management Versus Leadership

Listed below are characteristics of management versus leadership that typically show up in organizations. Add ones on either side that you observe within your organizations.

### MANAGEMENT VERSUS LEADERSHIP

| ▶ Managing (Will "kink the garden hose" to some significant degree if only managing.) | ▶ Leading (When balanced with managing, the greatest energy flow can occur.) |
|---|---|
| Efficiency. | Effectiveness. |
| How. | What and why. |
| Systems, procedures, policies, structure. | Trusting people. |
| Status quo. | Innovation and initiative. |
| Fixed. | Flexible. |
| Bottom-line. | Sees the possibilities along with the bottom line. |
| Aversion to risk. | Takes calculated risks. |
| Task oriented. | New directions. |
| More narrow in focus. | Focuses on big picture in balance with day to day. |
| Follows procedures and rules. | New ideas—sees the big picture. |
| Holds back when renewal needed. | Creative. |
| Handles all the details. | Continually reinvents the organization. |
| Reactive. | Inspires new vision. |
| Comfortable with status quo. | Makes leaps—proactive. |
| Resists change. | Change friendly. |
| Add your own observations: | Add your own observations: |

A true leader empowers people whenever possible. Telling is held to a minimum. True leaders inspire—they do not push people (including themselves). This motivates people by bringing them to identify with the task and the goal, rather than with their reward or punishment.

A true leader has the capacity to create a compelling vision that energizes people and results, moving them to a new place, and translating vision into appropriate strategies and actions. In healthy organizations, there is a true balance of management and leadership, for consistently getting the results organizations are striving for.

What is needed in every organization is more leadership, by more people. When this takes place, model organizations of success are born.

## Change without Resistance

"Change without resistance" is a phrase made popular by Doug Krug of Enlightened Leadership International. Client after client would deeply relate to the message within these words. We all face resistance to change to some degree. This book is focused on presenting what works in reducing (and possibly eliminating) resistance we, and those with whom we lead, have when facing change.

Through enhancing your personal leadership for greater freedom, you can thrive on change. Change is inevitable. We can create it proactively or it will *happen* to us.

### CHANGE WITHOUT RESISTANCE

| ▶ Change occurs because of: | ▶ The amount of change that brings the following results: |
|---|---|
| **Crisis:** A sudden, unexpected change | Cope, survive, some growth occurs (normally forced upon us) |
| **Evolution:** Changes over a long period of time | Life goes along just fine with some change and some goals realized |
| **Strategic objective:** Proactive changes occurring rapidly | Major investment (focus, time, energy) in continuous change results in accomplishing great things! |

Conclusion: Strategically create most of the changes in your life, thrive on those changes, generate results, and enjoy the fruits of your labors!

How can we and those with whom we lead become "change masters," even to the point of thriving on it?

First of all, what are your biggest current challenges to change?

| ▶ YOUR BIGGEST CURRENT CHALLENGES TO CHANGE | |
|---|---|
| ▶ Personally | ▶ In your organization |
| | |
| | |
| | |
| | |
| | |

All forms of resistance "kink the garden hose." Maintaining attitudes about the rapid changes in our lives becomes a very important focus. As we develop the attitude and practice of embracing changes, we are much more able to move through the adjustment phase more quickly, and so arrive at the desired results with minimal distractions. This is why the attitude of the "blessing of opposition" (change) is considered the foundation of continuous renewal.

Here are some simple suggestions for mastering change:
- Have the attitude that change is good. Eventually it will prove to be true.
- Trust that all change is given to us by "Life" to teach us and help us obtain what we want, despite what it looks like in the moment.
- Commit to an ongoing change program.
- Take responsibility for your own reactions to change.
- Get value from all the learnings from change.
- Always run on questions.
- When change is forced upon you by people or events, stay clear on who you are, believe in your self worth, and don't be drawn into the person (boss) or the event affecting you.

"People don't resist change, but being changed."   —DOUG KRUG

## Principle: Continuous Renewal/Change

**CONTINUOUS RENEWAL: FREEDOM STATEMENT POSSIBILITIES**

### Individual

"I am a person who embraces change. I am always looking for ways I can be better, in service to my own life's mission, and the lives of those around me. I pause frequently in my daily life to make sure I am moving in the direction I have chosen, while achieving the results I want. I contribute my very best to the organizations I am part of, in order to assist them with necessary changes whether they are created or just happen. My attitude about change is that it is good, and will always be for my best good in the long run, and the best for all involved. I am a truth seeker. I seek the truth for my unique life to direct my chosen path. I know that life supports me in getting what I want, and the needed changes and information along the way are made known to me in various ways to guide me. I stay 'awake' for the inevitable guideposts (truth) that lead me where I have chosen to go."

### Organization

"Our company is in a constant state of change, renewing itself all the time informally. In special retreats once every three months, we formally look at what is working, and what changes, additions, or deletions are needed to keep our momentum going. Our team thrives on change. We support the efforts of the individuals in our organization to always be innovative, creative, and looking for ways to improve. We are all change masters. We now see the dramatic changes that we create, or that are thrust on us from the outside world, as opportunities to work together and grow in achieving our desired results."

CHAPTER EIGHT: THRIVE ON CHANGE

## Attitude: The "Blessing" of Opposition

### OPPOSITION: FREEDOM STATEMENT POSSIBILITIES

**Individual**

"I accept opposition in my life as a blessing, because I know that life will always bring me those things that assist me in getting the results I desire, and that nothing will be given to me that I cannot handle. Love gets me through opposition, whatever form it comes in, and gratitude gets me through it quicker.

"I always run on the question of "What am I to learn from what is in my life right now?", and respond accordingly. I am better able to know and feel what is good in my life because of the opposition that shows up. Ultimately, I am a friend to change, internally and whatever happens externally in my life or in the world."

**Organization**

"Our organization focuses on what our desired results will look like. One of the reasons we have these goals is to help our people grow as the organization grows. Learning and applying those learnings is an important part of the process that enables us to achieve what we have chosen as our desired results. Therefore, top leadership embraces the attitude that the obstacles and changes we experience on the journey to achieve our goals are a natural, accepted part of the process, and are opportunities to learn and grow. We approach these challenges as a team, and value the input of all of our team members who choose to contribute. They are rewarded in many different ways, encouraging the involvement of the critical mass of our people in the exciting evolution of each other, and the world."

"That which we persist in doing becomes easier for us to do; not that the nature of the thing itself is changed, but that our power to do is increased."  —HEBER J. GRANT

What meaning does this quote have for you?

_____
_____
_____

As we persist in facing opposition in life with our principles, attitudes, and practices, "Life" promises us that the specific opposition will decrease in its magnitude in our life, until that moment comes when it is gone, and what is left is that we are stronger, and getting more of what we want in our lives.

## Practice: Running on Freedom Questions

> **RUNNING ON FREEDOM: STATEMENT POSSIBILITIES**
>
> "I know that the quality and quantity of "directions" and guidance I get in life to help me get the results I desire are directly related to the questions I am asking. I am always operating from written questions based on the needs I determine are important each day, all of which lead me to the realization of the vision I have for my life. I write down my questions in a journal and record what I receive as answers when they come. This is a real adventure for me.
>
> "My integrity is strong as I do exactly what I have been guided to do, thus opening my life up to even more guidance."

When organizations of all types practice operating from questions, such as those suggested in the previous freedom statement, and when they encourage their associates to provide personal leadership in doing the same within each of their areas of stewardship, true freedom to get desired results dramatically increases. What makes an effective question that is positive and focused (a "freedom question") is discussed in the next section of this chapter.

## The Infinite Freedom and Power of Questions

### POSITIVE-FOCUSED QUESTIONS—"FREEDOM QUESTIONS"

Freedom questions are the ultimate proactive source for getting answers to questions, and solutions to the challenges in your life, and in the life of all organizations. It is by far the most profound concept for progressing step by step, sometimes by leaps and bounds, towards accomplishing what is desired. Biblically, it has been said: "Ask, and ye shall receive."

Questions are so powerful because "Life" honors our free agency. It seems to be an unwritten law that normally Life will not force us to grow and change unless we choose to. Sometimes, things that just happen can cause tremendous change. These unexpected occurrences seem to be growing in power and frequency. But again, Life does not force us in how we will react even to these changes.

Questions open up the "garden hose" to having more energy come into our lives to help us in the ways for which we ask. It's almost like humility opens us up for answers and direction. However, the way questions are structured can have great impact for the "garden hose" being more open or more "kinked." The focus of the question, the "come from," has so much to do with the results we will get.

If the questions are negatively focused (create intimidation, are manipulative, or disempower us), then the "garden hose" naturally "kinks" and our ability to get desired results becomes so much more difficult. Here are some examples anyone can relate to:

- Why did you do that?
- Why did you do it that way?
- Why me?
- Why is this happening to me?
- What's wrong with you?
- What's the problem here?
- Why aren't you like him/her?
- Why aren't you getting more results?
- What's your problem?
- Why did they make me do that?
- What are we going to do about this problem?
- Don't you know better?
- Why aren't you keeping up?
- Why did you make that decision?

What do you notice about these questions?

_____
_____
_____

How do you feel reading through them?

___

___

___

We all have a choice. We can focus our attention and energy on all the reasons why we aren't achieving our desired results, or we can focus on what we have to do *in this moment* to accomplish what we choose to. As Enlightened Leadership International effectively states: "Whether people become part of the problem or part of the solution relates directly to the way we ask questions of ourselves and others."

Positive focused questions influence the effectiveness of getting answers and solutions, and it all relates to the amount of energy that is generated. Positive focused questions honor the opinions of others by their very nature and structure. They give a sense of equality—a powerful influence on people's willingness and ability to contribute.

Positive focused questions require expert listening skills to be at their highest level of success. Skills that are more from the heart than the head. They are non-judgmental by nature, and their essence is non-manipulative. They are not "why" questions—that makes people be naturally defensive. Read these positive focused questions:

- What can I do to support you?
- What else can I do?
- What has worked so far with this project?
- What does a good day look like for you?
- What needs to be done to achieve this?
- What are your desired results?
- What are the benefits of achieving this?
- What has been the value of this?
- What has been the best part of your day?

This last question deserves special attention, for it is an example of the real freedom and power of positive focused questions, ones that require more than a yes or no answer, and get positive results.

## DAVID'S STORY (FROM SANDRA JEAN PYNE)

My daughter and her four children had been living with me for nearly two years. She had been married to a man who severely abused their eight-year-old boy,

David. Since the father left, David has been a violent, disrespectful, non-caring, and sometimes suicidal child. When this behavior starts at six, it's frightening and challenging. Sometimes you just don't know what to do!

Shortly after they moved in with me, I began asking David the question, "What was the best thing that happened to you today?" "Nothing," was a typical reply. "I don't have anything good happen to me," would be another. Or silence.

I kept asking and getting nowhere. Then I decided to make the question, "What was the best thing that happened to you today?" our topic of discussion at the dinner table every night. Everyone discussed their day except David. Then one night he replied, "I'll tell you the worst thing that happened to me today."

At last a response! I asked him what was special about it. He was shocked, but he managed to find something small. I took that answer and built on it. By the time we were through he had something special in his day.

The next night when it was his turn, he found something "good" to talk about. It kept building each night. A month later, we sat down to dinner and the first thing out of David's mouth was, "Gramma, what was the best thing that happened to you today?" I was so excited! He had never asked the question before! A short time later, he came home from school and the moment he walked in the door, he asked his mother, "Mom, what is the best thing that has happened to you today, so far?" How exciting it was to hear David asking this question!

Along with other changes in his life, I know the power of this question is turning this little boy's life around. Instead of a seriously disturbed child, we now have a healthy, rambunctious—sometimes annoying—eight-year-old.

Appendix H: "Personal Leadership Questions," Appendix I: "Completing the Past Year and Preparing for the New Year," and Appendix N: "Freedom Questions" have many questions from many different disciplines in life for you to review. They are shared to inspire and encourage you to develop the unique questions for your own life and the lives who you have influence and association with.

How can properly structured questions be one of the most effective leadership tools for you?

_____
_____
_____

Enlightened Leadership International and Kurt Wright of Clear Purpose Management teach us that there are key elements in structuring questions so that the best answers, solutions, and thus results, are realized. They are:
- They begin with "what" and "how," not "why."
- They are non-judgmental.
- There is no intention to manipulate.
- They cannot be answered with a simple yes or no.
- They are stated in positive terms with positive words.
- They help people learn through the process of getting and giving answers.
- They are personalized, engaging people through honoring and uniting them rather than separating them.
- They show people that you are open and that you want to listen to the answers.
- They promote becoming an effective listener and encouraging and valuing all involved.

For getting more of the results we seek, it's time to take this truth to the deepest levels of our experience. To gain new information, we must ask a whole new world of questions.

What significant questions are in your life right now that you would like to focus on to get answers?

_____
_____
_____

What significant solutions are you focused on seeking to the challenges you are facing?

_____
_____
_____

How do these two questions relate to each of your organizations?

_____
_____
_____

## Practice: Personal Leadership Guidelines

> **PERSONAL LEADERSHIP: FREEDOM STATEMENT POSSIBILITY**
>
> "I effectively use the personal leadership guidelines to move through my personal and professional life with greater ease and flow for accomplishing the results I have chosen to achieve. I also use the guidelines for evolving objectives for me in all aspects of my life and for getting clearer about all the things that make my life work for me at the highest levels. It is exhilarating to have a structured way to increase the results I am able to achieve."

**PERSONAL LEADERSHIP GUIDELINES**

1. *Review/create desired results (objectives, goals, whatever you call your clear vision).*

   Constantly revise objectives and plans that are part of the renewal/change process, which can be very exciting as things evolve.

   Constantly increase clarity, giving "Life" a chance to find how to best support your efforts.

2. *What is the evidence that indicates I am moving towards my desired results?*

   Keep positively focused on the successes, great and small, that you realize. This approach produces greater freedom, rather than focusing on what is not working, what is causing you to be mired down with energy drain of focusing on all the problems. ("Problems" are worked at with guideline number six below after high energy is developed by focusing on numbers one to five.)

3. *What specifically generated this evidence?*

   Pause to reflect on what you are doing to create the successes you have noticed.

   Repeat those things that have been effective so that they can be repeated to get desired results easier and faster.

   Know why these things are effective so that others may learn from your experiences. Great stories can be gained and shared that will promote everyone's ability to accomplish more desired results.

   Remain very aware (a high level of awareness—one of the Attitudes that open the way to a high level of belief in yourself.)

*4. Revise desired results based on the insights discovered in guidelines two and three.*

Focus on the big picture (vision) or on the smallest project or desired result. This step and guideline number one draws together all the energy possible for building success, whether it be through other people or through other resources.

*5. What are the benefits to me personally by accomplishing this result?*

This guideline is a very important "why" question. Why am I seeking this desired result/goal/vision? The answer to this "why" question hopefully provides great fuel (strong feelings/emotions) for persisting until the desired result is achieved. It cannot be overemphasized enough—taking the time to thoroughly answer this question is a very important element of success. Make sure that this is not just an intellectual process. Make sure that you describe in detail the feelings, passion, and excitement that achieving this objective brings into your life, or the life of the organization.

Make sure that your mind (truth) and body (feelings) remain clear along the way so that when things get tough, there is the staying power to keep going. The sustained effort will be worthwhile.

Organizationally speaking, "buy-in," with as many people involved as possible, is an important aspect for maintaining sustained high energy throughout the journey of achievement. It is the added fuel to keep the fires going.

*6. What can I now do additionally, or what can I improve on, or possibly do differently to move even closer to what I desire to achieve?*

The challenges, obstacles, and problems encountered, can be discussed with much more creativity and energy when this question follows one through five. Solutions often become more apparent.

Come up with action plans that have worked and more that need to be done, or adjust plans based on the learnings.

Chapter ten discusses how to "stay on a roll." These first six steps are great tools that keep the roll going long after the "being on a roll" has started.

*7. What specifically can I do, by when?*

This is the basis for being accountable (a key to getting desired results faster) and creates real stewardship. It also brings clarity once the big picture has been created, by determining the first and subsequent steps for achieving success.

*8. How will I measure my progress?*

Having a standard to measure success is very important to being clear on what is desired. When progress is measured, progress improves.

9. *Who will I be accountable to?*

This is a great opportunity for both people involved to grow in relationship to each other in a positive and healthy way that strives to accomplish desired bottom line results. Chapter Four describes the importance of this person in your life.

What has been the greatest value for you with this material?

_____
_____
_____

What areas in your personal and professional life can you see this working?

_____
_____
_____

Personal Leadership guidelines are an excellent tool that uses properly structured questions for solving problems and keeping projects moving forward as best as possible. It aids conflict management, personal progress reporting, and in an infinite number of ways benefits you personally and the organizations you are part of.

Pause and copy the form on the next page (or create your own) and fill one out for all your desired results.

Desired result title: _____  Date _____

Desired result in detail: _____
_____
_____

What has been effective? _____
_____
_____

What is making it effective? _____
_____
_____

What revisions are needed to the desired result? _____
_____
_____

What are the benefits? (What's in it for me?) _____
_____
_____

What can I now do additionally, improve upon, or do differently? _____
_____
_____

What will I do, by when? _____
_____
_____

How will I know I'm succeeding? _____
_____
_____

To whom am I accountable? _____
_____
_____

CHAPTER EIGHT: THRIVE ON CHANGE

## THE POWER OF THESE PRACTICES IN BUSINESS

"It ain't braggin' if ya done it."   —DIZZY DEAN

Kurt Wright of Clear Purpose Management tells of the following experience: A $100 million dollar software development project for the Canadian government was 18 months behind schedule with only 10 months to go on the contract. Being even one day late caused a $3 million dollar penalty. When a "critical mass" of the team of 400 people implemented the concepts and tools taught in this section, they finished the project in nine months, one month ahead of schedule, on budget, and with the desired quality.

The freedom and power of positive focused questions aligns the hearts, minds, and strengths of teams.

## Practice: Listening with the Heart

> **LISTENING WITH HEART: FREEDOM STATEMENT POSSIBILITY**
>
> "I am an excellent listener, with my heart and my ears. I keep my mind quiet in seeking Divine guidance when listening to others. This way I remain open to what is the highest truth for the greatest good in the moment. I stay present with those who are speaking to me."

In order to help you get to a deeper understanding and application of the listening skills that produce greater desired results (leadership!), here are some suggestions:

When someone is speaking, listen intently rather than allowing your mind to be distracted with other concerns. Remain present with the person.

Be patient, not anxious, to "get your turn to speak."

As Stephen R. Covey teaches, "Seek first to understand, then to be understood," so that we do not listen to agree or disagree based on our own values and perceptions. In other words, no interpretation, prejudice, expectations, or anticipating the answers. Do not judge what is being said based upon how it fits into your existing belief structure. Pure listening with the heart, never judges something said as right or wrong, good or bad.

- Listen with nothing else on your mind. Focus on the person only, and what is being shared.
- Listen with real empathy and understanding. Ask questions that help in the understanding of what is being said, but not questions that put the person on the defensive as discussed earlier in this chapter.
- Listen with a quiet, open mind.

It is powerful to sincerely be open to new perspectives in your life. That opens you up to listen to others without having them feel like you are judging them.

In working with the Divine, and with other people, such listening really facilitates the "thriving on change" results. Using questions in your life, listening with the heart (and not the head) are the keys to achieving more results, faster and definitely easier.

## What It Takes To Make a Major Change

Life will either bring us things that force major change (loss of job, accident) or we can choose to proactively make the changes that improve our lives and the lives of those around us.

Let's assume you are choosing to make a major change. The twelve steps outlined in Chapter Three are the foundation steps. Listed below are additional suggestions in being successful with the more challenging results we go after, or the apparent stumbling blocks that come upon you:

- Know and trust that life supports you in your choices for good. Somehow things are drawn to you for achieving all that you want to accomplish.
- Focus on "feeling" the worth and value to you in achieving your desired results. Feelings of the body provide an energy that is very powerful when accompanied by appropriate thoughts.
- As stated earlier, scientific research has proven that the body cannot tell the difference between something vividly imagined and something that is actually experienced. Visualization is a very powerful tool for attaining the highest levels of human achievement.
- When you stand at that inevitable edge—when something, someone, some emotion/mood, or any such distraction is trying to move you away from achieving your desired results—this is when the greatest opportunity for growth and success comes. It is a time to not falter if

at all possible, but to stand up straight, and stand forth with your dreams alive in your heart (feelings) and mind (clear image).
- Take a deep breath and accept the feelings of rejection, resistance, fear of the unknown, being judged, or any turmoil that may be a part of this moment on the edge. Step forward and do what you know to do. Take action! Take that leap of faith and reap the rewards of your faith, in yourself, and in what you have desired.
- Sometimes it feels like you are toe-to-toe with all the darkness of failure, facing it with only the light of your success. The edge is purposeful. It is your opportunity to make your greatest progress, and even possibly to receive your accomplished desires, and your greatest learnings. This may sound unbelievable, but once you have successfully experienced the edge, you will get to the point when new "edges" are welcomed.
- Stop, be aware, and celebrate your success all along the way.

## THE GARDEN HOSE: KINKING VERSUS FLOWING

▶ **"Kinking the Garden Hose"**
**(Desired results harder to get)**

▶ **"Energy Flowing"**
**(Desired results come easier, quicker, and more abundantly)**

| "Kinking the Garden Hose" | "Energy Flowing" |
|---|---|
| 1. Hate. | 1. Love. |
| 2. Not authentic. | 2. Thankfulness. |
| 3. Fear. | 3. Courage. |
| 4. Egotism. | 4. Humility. |
| 5. Resist change. | 5. Welcomes change as a natural process in life. |
| 6. Negative attitude. | 6. Positive attitude. |
| 7. Reactive. | 7. Proactive. |
| 8. Avoids opposition. | 8. Accepts opposition. |
| 9. Critical of self/others. | 9. Honors self/others. |
| 10. Wants to change others. | 10. Accepts others as they are. |
| 11. Blame others. | 11. Self-responsibility. |

Add others that come up for you:
_____
_____

Add others that come up for you:
_____
_____

What has been of greatest value to you from reading this chapter?

_____
_____
_____

Is there something specific that you want to add to your desired results because of this value?

_____
_____
_____

Is it worth power pausing now to complete a plan for the added result?
___ Yes ___ No

If yes, copy the Change Master Plan form (page 164) and create your future now.

_____
_____
_____

What will be your "I am" freedom statement to support your plan?

**Today, By Choice, I Am…**

_____
_____
_____
_____

CHAPTER EIGHT: THRIVE ON CHANGE

# 9
# THE KEY TO FREEDOM

"Integrity is the key to your power."  —STEPHEN R. COVEY

**Principle: Integrity**

---

### INTEGRITY: FREEDOM STATEMENT POSSIBILITIES

**Individual** ↙    ↘ **Organization**

"I am a person who continuously strives to think, say, and do who I have chosen to be. What I say I will do, I do, for I enjoy making and keeping all my commitments. In organizations I am associated with, I give my best to know and live by their guiding Principles. I focus on being obedient to those things I have been asked to do, and that I have been guided to do. When I am clear what I need to do, I live by the words 'do it!' As truth that I have accepted as mine comes into my life, I consciously work at integrating it until it becomes a part of my thinking, feeling, speaking, and behavior."

"One of our organization's primary focuses is 'walking our talk.' We have taken the time to be clear on who we are and what we want to accomplish, and how we will get there while revising both as necessary. We have communicated it to all of our team members throughout our company, and we repeat the communications often. We maintain awareness that makes sure that all of our team members speak and act according to our values. We constantly hold meetings simply to review our progress, especially using the Personal Leadership guidelines. Our integrity is of paramount importance to us, as shown by our words and actions."

## Attitude: Obedience

In terms of continuously succeeding at enlarging the "garden hose" and increasing the flow of energy for greater success, obedience is truly the attitude (and practice) that brings the greater value. When we are guided to what our next steps for achievement of desired results are, and then we are trusting and obedient to those thoughts and feelings, greater freedom comes. "Life" seems to reward our faith, trust, and obedience. As a result, more guidance is given, which brings us closer to our achievements.

What is your current level of power to be obedient to what you know is true for you?

_____
_____
_____

Is this an important attitude for you? Is it time to now power pause and get recommitted to how you plan your life so that the power of being obedient continually grows in you and in your organizations?

_____
_____
_____

Obedience is a significant factor in enlarging the "garden hose" in our lives for more momentum to build. It is the one thing, above all the other things that have been said in this book, that the author has personally struggled with the most. It delayed results and restricted additional answers to questions I had because I had not gone forth with the guidance I had already received. Guidance often is a step by step process with "Life" guiding us along the way. "Life" will wait patiently for the next step to actually be taken in, learned, and applied before the next step can be given. Obedience is a central part of our integrity.

CHAPTER NINE: THE KEY TO FREEDOM

### OBEDIENCE: FREEDOM STATEMENT POSSIBILITIES

| Individual ↙ | ↘ Organization |
|---|---|
| "I am a person who lives by what I believe. I know that through being obedient and true to what I know, that true freedom, not bondage, will increase. I take great pleasure in my power to live the life I now choose to live. Being true to what I believe brings me great freedom and joy in life to accomplish all that I desire. When I get thoughts and feelings of what I need to do next, I am able to immediately respond and DO IT!" | "Our organization understands the importance of being obedient to those principles and values that we have determined meet our specific needs for accomplishing our desired results. We are disciplined as an organization, and adhere to what we believe. We spend appropriate time, energy, and resources making sure that our team members think, feel, speak, and act in concert with our vision and mission statements." |

## Practice: Making and Keeping Commitments

The Practice of consciously making commitments and then keeping them builds confidence and self esteem. First and foremost is to do it with yourself. For example, we have all heard and experienced first hand New Year's resolutions—a new decision is made and gone with for awhile, then something happens that weakens our ability to follow through.

Depending on where you are with this Principle of integrity, do many small things you've promised to do, and do them consistently, developing a positive habit pattern of obedience: Be aware this is happening, that you are succeeding, and then celebrate your accomplishments. This will grow as you gain experience and confidence. Doing this with others is more risky, but the value will increase your power to maintain absolute integrity. Doing this in small ways will build your power to do it in significant areas of your life, until it becomes a very powerful pattern of your life. The results you consistently get in life will magnify that much more.

There is incredible energy and freedom (power) in a promise. Promises take you out of being a spectator of life. Words in the form of a promise become actions that have a tremendous impact on your life, the lives of your organizations, and the world. In fulfilling your promises, you create a condition that supports getting your results, rather than being distracted by emotions and moods. Those who make and keep commitments consistently, distinguish themselves as true leaders in the world, no matter what their so-called status in life is. You will find yourself producing consistent results. Such experience creates freedom, joy, confidence, and the power to accelerate new chosen desires.

Another very important part of this process for strengthening your integrity with this practice is that, as long as your desires are sincere in being a person of high integrity, when you seemingly "fail" at doing something you promised to do, feel it for a moment, then forgive yourself. Address the needs of those who were affected and then let it go. Again, see the feeling and thought as a little butterfly and see it fly away, never to return.

Remember, letting go is an important part of the change process for expediting the results you want. Forgive as quickly as possible, and as often as words, acts, thoughts, and feelings that do not support your commitment come up. Go back to the truth, either mentally or what you have previously written down in your "I am…" freedom statement, and review it and repeat it a few times. Always keep the truth of what you are seeking in your thoughts. Always let go when you do not live up to your new truths. It will speed up the process.

Also, remember that playing is an important part of accelerating results, so make sure you reward yourself when a promise is made and kept. This can be as simple as acknowledging yourself.

Always maintain faith in yourself to succeed and the courage to get back up again after the illusion of "failing" has occurred. Persist until you are consistently successful.

**CASUAL COMMITMENT**

A casual commitment lets life slip by, and will not work in accomplishing your goals, especially if the goals stretch you into new levels of performance from your current life achievements. All the areas that you choose to follow up on and implement from studying this book need your constant care and attention, each and every day. Hopefully it will become a passion for you, if it isn't already. Life demands a real commitment, in order for us to thrive and even survive.

What is your commitment level, and what does it look like for the things you are choosing to be, do and enjoy in your life?

_____
_____
_____

Now, create a symbol (see Chapter Ten) that will remind you of this commitment.

_____
_____
_____

What has been of greatest value to you from reading this chapter?

_____
_____
_____

### THE GARDEN HOSE: KINKING VERSUS FLOWING

| ▶ "Kinking the Garden Hose" (Desired results harder to get) | ▶ "Energy Flowing" (Desired results come easier, quicker, and more abundantly) |
|---|---|
| 1. My word does not align with my actions. | 1. Word equals Deed. |
| 2. I don't seem to do what I believe is my next step. | 2. When I know what I need to do, I do it! |
| 3. I don't keep promises. | 3. I make and keep all my commitments. |
| 4. My beliefs do not equal my word and actions. | 4. I live and speak from my beliefs. |

Add others that come up for you:

_____
_____

Add others that come up for you:

_____
_____

Is there something specific that you want to add to your desired results because of this value?

_____
_____
_____

Is it worth power pausing now to complete a plan for the added result?
___ Yes ___ No

If yes, copy the Change Master Plan form (page 164) and create your future now.

_____
_____
_____

What will be your "I am" freedom statement to support your plan?

**Today, By Choice, I Am...**

_____
_____
_____
_____

CHAPTER NINE: THE KEY TO FREEDOM

# 10
# "STAYING ON A ROLL"—KEEPING THE MOMENTUM GOING

**Principle: Balance**

Here are seven qualities of America's achievers, from a national magazine study of 1500 people:
1. Lead a well balanced life.
2. Select a career they care about.
3. Rehearse each challenging task mentally (with feelings aroused).
4. Seek results, not perfection.
5. Be willing to risk.
6. Don't underestimate themselves or their potential.
7. Compete with yourself—not others.

## BALANCE: FREEDOM STATEMENT POSSIBILITIES

### Individual ↙   ↘ Organization

"I am a balanced person, enjoying the fruits of balance (peace, calmness, emotional health, physical fitness, mental clarity) each day. I pause frequently throughout the day for brief moments, and pause more on the weekend, to make sure I remain in balance. I consistently focus attention on all areas of my life that I consider to be important to be a balanced person. I enjoy the freedom that comes, through balance, in getting the results I choose for my life, and for my consistent ability to contribute more effectively to the organizations I am part of."

(Note: See Appendix J, "Twelve Areas of Balance" for a suggested list of the areas of life to be balanced.)

"We balance our need for bottom line results with honoring, valuing, and nurturing each and every person in our organization who helps generate those results. We allow our team members to discover ways to have appropriate fun during the work day. We support, where possible, programs that support the family life needs of our team members. We allow our team to do with their workspace things that are meaningful to them, that nurture them, without being inappropriate to those whom we serve. We allow them to decorate the office with appropriate fun and seasonal decorations. We also have provided plants throughout our office that bring some balance to their lives at work. We balance between having our team members accountable for results with training and other things that support their personal and professional life, which generates greater success for all."

(Note: The list of things that could be a part of this freedom statement seem infinite. Each organization should take the time to evaluate what works best for them, including asking their people for input.)

CHAPTER TEN: STAYING ON A ROLL

The Ford Foundation's study of organizations is important for achieving further clarity about a company's need to be more in balance with the personal and professional life of their people. As the business world continues to do whatever it takes to achieve bottom line financial results, a powerful message comes from this study to assist them.

The vision and predictions for the business world in the new millennium is that there will be unprecedented results achieved by many companies. It will take personal leadership from all of the people within the organizations, and the organizations themselves must be aware of their people and serve them by helping them realize the very best that is within them.

The customer is normally the number one focus. The new awareness that is picking up momentum is that "Yes, the customer is an important focus, but it is the organization's own people, those who connect with the customer, that need the number one attention and focus." (Ford Foundation study)

The study is entitled *Relinking Life and Work: Toward a Better Future*. It is a study based on a collaborative research project with Xerox Corporation, Tandem Computers, and Corning, Inc. that took place over a seven year period.

"The Ford Foundation's groundbreaking study… sends an important message to our nation's business leaders. The project began with the belief that changes in work practices that were designed to make work and the workplace more family-friendly could be accomplished with no loss to business productivity. But this view underestimates the benefits of a work-family approach. The research shows that this approach offers companies a strategic opportunity to achieve a more equitable and a more productive workplace. Individual energy and creativity are unleashed when changes in work practices benefit employee's personal lives. At a time when corporate America is being assailed for putting profits above all else, it is gratifying that this study has established that the best business strategy recognizes that greater employee satisfaction means greater productivity and, in turn, better business results."

In the early 1990s companies made efforts to pay more attention to the personal life of their people, but there was a large gap between the promises of flexible policies and programs to help employees and the actual implementation, which fell far short. Companies deep down inside were less than confident that efforts to integrate work and personal lives would not eventually have negative consequences to their bottom line.

In large companies, major organizational change takes somewhere between eight and ten years. It's possible that they were unwilling to pay the price and take the risk. Companies still operate with the paradigm that employees will make work their top concern. Generally speaking, it will not happen in the long run. The same Ford Foundation study came to the following four important discoveries:

1. The separation of work and family undermines both business and employee goals, impairing work efficiency and family life.

2. The process of challenging old assumptions and cultural beliefs that underlie work and work-family integration frees employees to think more creatively about work and provides companies with a strategic opportunity to achieve a more equitable, productive, and innovative workplace.
3. Many of the same assumptions and beliefs that create difficulties in work-family integration also lead to unproductive work practices, undermining the companies' ability to achieve key business goals.
4. Restructuring the way work gets done to address work-family integration can lead to positive "win-win" results—a more responsive work environment takes employees' needs into account, yields significant bottom line results.

The study shows that work practices and employer expectations, continue to be based on the notion that employees should be willing and able to make work their top priority.

However, Personal Leadership is based on the underlying assumption that our greatest success in achieving unheard of results as organizations will come as each individual steps up to the challenge of bringing more of their best to life through the process of personal change. Organizations who support and give attention in word and deed to that effort, will achieve consistent and abundant success unparalleled in the history of business, successes that any organization can realize. Separation of professional and personal life in all the important areas for a person, as reaffirmed in the Ford study, will disintegrate over time.

The new millennium will continue to bring a greater unifying of the human race in the realization mentally, and the experience physically, of our full potential as individuals and organizations. This chapter's intent is to help individuals in contributing their current best, as it is always evolving and increasing, to each organization that they are part of. It is also the intent of this chapter to assist organizations in going deeper, with greater commitment, in allowing this to take place.

## Attitude: Positive Focus

### POSITIVE FOCUS: FREEDOM STATEMENT POSSIBILITIES

**Individual**

"I look positively at life, and all that happens to me. The glass is half full, not half empty. I focus on being my best, and the best in all people in my life. I am solution focused, not problem oriented. I don't ignore problems, but focus immediately on how to bring answers for a solution. I experience life as an adventure, and not as drudgery. I see what is working in my life, and build upon that."

**Organization**

"All the people in our organization know from experience that our results come faster, easier, and more abundantly as we stay positive, no matter what outside influences or internal challenges come our way. When challenges come, we unite with the appropriate people and look for solutions. We are constantly asking what have we learned from this experience, whether it be really positive or so-called negative. We then implement what we have learned as part of our ongoing renewal/change program. We have eliminated thoughts, feelings, emotions, words, and actions that make something wrong or bad. In this way we are continually on a roll towards accomplishing our desired results."

(Note: See Chapter Eight for how the personal leadership guidelines functions as a tool in developing more of your capacity to live with this Attitude.)

### FAILURE IS AN ILLUSION

Chapter Seven showed that by "resetting the zero," there are no weaknesses, only degrees of strength. Similarly, there are no failures, and with the right attitude, there are only degrees of success. As a minimum, our learnings from our so-called failures are our success for generating more of what we want in our life in the future. In truth, failure is an illusion. Failure is a false reality because we measure failure as a degree of success. This is far more than a positive mental attitude. Life flows smoother and easier when we measure everything by some degree of success, making more "Life" available to accomplish our desired results.

Thoughts generate energy. The same illusion about failure holds true about negative thoughts. In truth, there are no thoughts that bring negative energy to our bodies. "Negative" thoughts are in fact thoughts that have zero or minimal energy. Thus, we do not move forward in our achievements. The following illustration symbolizes two people (person A and person B) with their accumulated thoughts over some period of time. (%) equals one moment, one minute, one hour, one day, of accumulated thoughts, with "o" being zero energy focused thoughts and "+" being positive. In person A, 80 percent of their thoughts over a period of time are focused on what's wrong—problems, low esteem, being critical, anger, things are bad, complaining (zero energy thoughts)—and 20 percent on positive thoughts. Person B is the opposite.

**THOUGHTS GENERATE ENERGY**

▶ Person A: Focused on What's Wrong       ▶ Person B: Focused on What's Right

| 0%            | 80%  | 100% | 0% | 20%        | 100% |
|---------------|------|------|----|------------|------|
| o o o o o     | +    |      | o  | + + + + +  |      |
| oooooooooooo  |      |      | o  | + + + + + ++ |    |
| ooooooo       | +    |      | o  | + + + + + ++ |    |
| oooooooooooo  | +    |      | o  | ++++++++   |      |

To accomplish our desired results faster, easier, and to gain more of them, we need to choose powerful thoughts (like the freedom statements) that support the achievement of our desires. The more focused we can stay with our positive thoughts, the greater energy levels for freedom to successfully achieve our hearts desires (and the accumulated thoughts of all team members in an organization towards the goals of that organization). The power of two or more holding positive thoughts towards a common goal generate the unheard of results that successful organizations in the future are destined to realize.

Since who we are, and what results we get, are directly related to the accumulated thoughts we choose or just allow to come into our mind, which person is likely to be happier and more of an achiever of desired results?

____ A?____ B?

Which person would likely have a more "kinked garden hose" and which one more open to getting desired results? Why?

_____
_____
_____

Which person would naturally be more open to new ideas and creativity? Why?

_____
_____
_____

Suggestions:
    Be in control of what you think about, as much as possible.
    Choose positive focused thoughts.
    Keep focused on your desired results.

## Attitude: Play

Being forward focused when clarity is determined, keeps the "garden hose" flowing freely. Similar results occur with play! If you are mentally asleep after having made new choices and decisions, it "kinks the garden hose" for getting results.

Stephan Sivey and Jerome and Dorothy Singer, psychologists from Yale University, found that dopamine levels (which are helpful for neural plasticity, and aid in learning and creativity) are increased during play. Stress inhibits the learning process. To prove the point about play, look at the word "stressed." *Stressed is desserts spelled backwards!*

Now that is seeing and creating with a playful eye.

> **PLAY: FREEDOM STATEMENT POSSIBILITIES**
>
> **Individual** ↙  ↘ **Organization**
>
> "I enjoy all aspects of my life. I play frequently in many different ways. I know about and have experienced the benefits of play to creativity in my life, and for my emotional, mental, and physical well being. I even enjoy being playful at work, and we as a team get a lot more accomplished when we take brief moments to play. I have also increased my learning capacity as I have looked at life more playfully."
>
> "Our organization has allowed our team members to get out of the box and create ways to play at work. As a result, we are consistently getting more of the results we want, evidence of the power of balance at work through play. Looking at the lighter side of life is a major contributor to the creativity and innovation we experience in our organization."

In the next Practice, some of the evidence in the value of play is reviewed. The numerous forms play can take varies with the number of people in the organization. Take time to power pause, as an individual, and as an organization, to determine what would be appropriate and beneficial to do consistently.

What is your level of "buy in" to the power of play?  ___ High ___ Low

If your answer is "high," take time to ponder the following question: In what ways will you increase the power of playing in your own life?

_____
_____
_____

## Practice: The Four C's for Sustainable Growth

Being "on a roll" holds the belief that the only sure thing about being "on a roll" is that it will end. But there is a tool to apply that assures greater success for sustaining the "roll."

### 1. Clarity

As stated many times before, it is vital to always stay clear with what you want and what you believe. Your vision of the results you want will change frequently. (Many individuals and companies lose momentum with visions because they spend a lot of time and energy on creating them, but very little effort on giving time to constantly review and revise.) This concept can be as big as a vision for life accomplishments, or as simple as a new decision being made. For example, you may choose to adopt a new attitude of gratitude as a next step in your progress.

### 2. Choice

The choices in life are limitless, but it does take action on your part in making the choices of what results you desire, and the decisions about how you will get there. Always remain at choice with life, either with what you create, or how you will react to what comes into your life.

### 3. Consciousness

Also as stated earlier, awareness is a very powerful key to personal and organizational progress. The more aware we become, the more abundant and faster our results will come to us.

*Noticing when progress is being made with your vision, and constantly making new decisions, will accelerate more progress.* Momentum builds faster when progress is noticed. It's exciting to watch the power of this process work.

(Note: When things are not moving in the right direction, go back to the clarity and choices that have been made and make sure they still make sense and feel like it is still the right direction. If they do, then persist and keep looking for all small and great signs that progress is being made.)

### 4. Celebration

This is a fun habit. Doing it with others makes this part of the process increase the joy of life and work. Some of the suggested ways to celebrate are:

Take time to express an acknowledgment that something has happened to show progress.

Express gratitude quietly in your own mind, verbally to someone or your team in the organization, or by writing in a gratitude journal. A journal for doing this has been gaining popularity. Enlightened Leadership International calls a "hall meeting" with everyone who is in the office. They gather around and the one who is "noticing" tells what happened. Everyone gets to participate and share in the celebration.

Enlightened Leadership International also uses a "win" board where successes are written down and posted on big Post-it notes so everyone receives the communication when they come into the office.

Play increases our energy flow. When experienced in balance with the other aspects of life, play increases the energy in accomplishing results, and makes the journey more enjoyable. Play can take on many forms, and be as short or long as seems appropriate for the circumstances. But when a major goal or result is achieved, it would be well worth it to spend some significant time and money on the celebration. It engages us and others in the joy of accomplishment.

## Practice: The Power of Symbols

"...Successful performance is directly related to the power of concentration, to the will, to the desire, to total interest and involvement. The person has to be excited. Then he (she) can do amazing things. But if the interest and concentration are not kept at a high level, nothing much goes on. When the level is high, the mind actually has a direct effect on things. The mind can do astonishing things just by thought. It is a matter of concentrating and ordering it.

"(Symbols) direct, concentrate, discipline, and inform the thought. To be effective, thought must be so motivated and directed."
—HUGH NIBLEY

Symbols are very powerful in terms of helping us get what we want. Here are three steps for using symbols.
1. Choose symbols to remind you of the goals, or activities, that you have chosen to accomplish.
2. Put the symbols in a place where you will see them frequently each day.
3. Pause as frequently as possible and be reminded in thought *and* feeling the accomplishment of your goals.

There are things we can choose in our lives, and in our organizations, that will quickly and easily remind us of our vision, the desired results we seek, and keep the feelings alive about what it feels like to achieve those results. These things remind us of how to feel and behave when times are tough, or they just remind us to keep the energy flowing about our dreams. Symbols are a reminder that we want to do certain things that we know will get the results we want. A symbol can be a mental image as well as a tangible object (although if it's not tangible it can be too easy to forget). Play with symbols and see what works for you.

The United States has a very powerful symbol of the eagle that symbolizes freedom. When we look at an eagle and pause for a moment, it brings back feelings we have of our freedom in a free country.

A stop sign is a symbol to keep our behavior consistent with protecting our lives and the lives of others on the road.

McDonalds has made use of the power in symbols by having the golden arches all over the world. People have immediate thoughts, feelings, and behaviors when they see that symbol in ads or on the streets.

Experience the power of symbols to keep you on track as you get clear about which ones make sense for you. Then spend a moment (five seconds to five minutes), frequently, to look at the symbol. This will have an important impact on your freedom to get results. Over time, the energy for accomplishment will increase through simply using symbols. The only way to know if this is true is to try it. The increased freedom to get results is in direct proportion to your experience with what is true for you. Symbols quickly help us to remember thoughts/experiences of achieving our goals.

Here is a personal application story: There is the experience of a man who wanted to have more of the noble and loving characteristics of a person that he honored, respected, and loved in his life. It was a spiritual leader who had profound influence over this man's life. He had a picture (another example of a symbol) of this man on a wall in his house. Each morning the man would stop and just stand there and look at his spiritual leader. He would just let the thoughts and feelings come forth and experience the noble character of this leader who had an incredible ability to love unconditionally. He expressed that just this small practice, for five minutes a day, was having a profound effect at his desired results of having a more noble and loving character.

What "buy in" do you have for this concept of the power of symbols?

_____
_____
_____

Is the "buy in" sufficient to apply this to your life and experience the difference? If yes, what symbols make sense for you as you review your desired results? Is a collage using multiple symbols or a scrapbook of the future possible fun projects for you to create?

_____
_____
_____

Everything presented in this book is designed for you to create more freedom for the desired results you want, and to get them faster and easier. Your application of symbols may be the only separation between the truth of this concept and it making a difference in achieving greater personal leadership in your life.

Selecting symbols and putting them in places where they can be frequently looked at are only two-thirds of the steps to using symbols. That two-thirds represents only five percent of the power of symbols. True freedom comes when we pause and remember with the mind and feel in the body what the symbol represents to us. If we have a profound experience that has brought significant truth (mind) and feelings (body) for getting or moving closer to desired results, then reviewing the experience again and again can be very powerful. A symbol can help us remember. Try it! Prove for yourself this source of freedom.

CHAPTER TEN: STAYING ON A ROLL

## THE GARDEN HOSE: KINKING VERSUS FLOWING

▶ **"Kinking the Garden Hose"**
(Desired results harder to get)

1. Forgetting goals or promises made to get results.
2. Not clear what we want.
3. Not frequently reviewing what we want and our plans.
4. Not directing our life and the lives of organizations we are part of.
5. Unconscious—not working for small successes that lead to big successes.
6. Letting small steps go unnoticed and unappreciated.

Add others that come up for you:
_____
_____
_____

▶ **"Energy Flowing"**
(Desired results come easier, quicker, and more abundantly)

1. Using symbols as reminders.
2. Clear vision, mission, goals.
3. Continuous attention on goals and evolving them as appropriate.
4. Choosing and constantly making new choices about desired results.
5. Looking for each small and great step towards ultimate achievement of desired results.
6. Celebrating small and large successes.

Add others that come up for you:
_____
_____
_____

What has been of greatest value to you from reading this chapter?
_____
_____
_____

Is there something specific that you want to add to your desired results because of this value?
_____
_____
_____

Is it worth power pausing now to complete a plan for the added result?
___ Yes ___ No

If yes, copy the Change Master Plan form (page 164) and create your future now.

_____
_____

What will be your "I am" freedom statement to support your plan?

**Today, By Choice, I Am...**

_____
_____
_____
_____

# 11

# FREEDOM FOR EXPERIENCING ALL AND MORE OF DESIRED RESULTS

**Principle: Law of the Harvest**

> **LAW OF THE HARVEST: FREEDOM STATEMENT POSSIBILITY**
>
> "I give to life what I have chosen to have in my life. It is called the 'Law of the Harvest.' Whatever I want in my life, I give it first, then I receive it back and more! I know this law is infinite, so that the more I give, the more I receive."

This powerful Principle is also referred to as the law of cause and effect, the law of action and reaction, or karma. References in the holy scriptures refer to it as the Law of the Harvest: Everything multiplies after its own kind. All of life reveals this truth.

The law holds true for plants, birds, fish, insects, animals, and people. If you plant a watermelon seed, you won't get a tomato. If you want a tomato you will have to plant the right kind of seed. A seed does not just return one seed and does not remain just a planted seed. It multiplies after its own kind. This is a significant understanding.

If you plant a watermelon seed and nourish it, it will grow into a melon vine with several watermelons, each containing hundreds of seeds. A kernel of corn does not return just a single kernel of corn. The conception of a child results in a future father or mother, a grandfather or grandmother.

When you apply this Principle to daily life situations, you will discover that it also applies to our thoughts, feelings, and actions.

Frederick Babbel tells the following:

"In one of the training courses I directed at the National Archives, we had several personnel attending from the US Navy's David Taylor Model Basin, near Washington DC. Since we were considering the principles and practices of good management, I discussed this concept (the law of cause and effect) with them as it applied to their specific functions and activities.

"One of the students challenged my suggestion that our thoughts and feelings are projected to those around us and would likewise result in an increased return of good or ill. He and his companions volunteered to conduct an experiment to prove that I was mistaken about such things. I invited them to bring their results to the concluding session two weeks later.

"When they returned, they sketched briefly on the blackboard a diagram of their experiment. They had taken a piece of heavy plank, and on top of it they had mounted a seismograph. Underneath they had suspended a sonar sounding device like that used on ships to detect underwater disturbances.

"They placed this equipment well out in one of their man-made lakes. Then they took a large boulder and threw it so it landed in the water near this device. The seismograph registered the splash, the waves, and even the ripples as they disappeared along the shoreline.

"The students continued to focus their binoculars on the seismograph. In a little while the recording needle began to move in an ever-increasing intensity. The monitoring tape showed the final register to be almost three times the intensity of the register of the splash.

"They concluded that the ripples to the shoreline had returned under water back to the rock, the original source of the energy. The sonar system in the water indicated that the force that returned to the rock had been multiplied approximately three times.

"They concluded that since the principle applied to inanimate objects (such as the rock), it would surely apply to thoughts and feelings, which scientific instruments have recorded as producing measurable amounts of energy."

Whatever we give to the world through our thoughts, feelings, emotions, words spoken, actions, and behaviors, we get back three times and more. If we have a poor attitude, we will get that back in our life. If we show love, we will receive love back through many sources that Life can provide.

What do you want more of in your life?

_____
_____
_____

Are you willing to give it first? ____ Yes ____ No

If yes, what changes in your written desired results do you need to make to achieve more of what you want?

_____
_____
_____

## Attitude: Gratitude

> **GRATITUDE: FREEDOM STATEMENT POSSIBILITY**
>
> "I am grateful for all things in my life and express it frequently and openly. I tell people thank you when they do or say things for my benefit. I write notes of thanks often for good deeds done to me or observed doing for others. Each night I record in a journal the things that I have been grateful for that day. I simply acknowledge people when I see them being good, doing good things, and succeeding in what results they are looking for in their lives."

Obviously there are many Practices that have been suggested in the above freedom statement. Likely, there are many that are not included that are unique to your desires. If you choose gratitude as one of your Attitudes, then select the Practices that work for you. But before deciding if this one fits for you, consider the following:

"Gratitude is deeper than thanks. Thankfulness is the beginning of gratitude. Gratitude is the completion of thankfulness. Thankfulness may consist in fully of words. Gratitude is shown in acts..."
—DAVID O. MCKAY

"Understand that (any physical) healing can take considerable time—it is accelerated when gratitude is expressed to God for every degree of improvement noted." —RICHARD G. SCOTT

"In some quiet way, the expression and feelings of gratitude have a wonderful cleansing or healing nature. Gratitude brings warmth to the giver and the receiver alike." —ROBERT D. HALES

Assuming you "buy in" to this Attitude as a way to achieve your desired results, and more, what specific things are you willing to do in applying this to your daily life? To the life of the organizations you are part of?

_____
_____
_____

## Practice: Service to People and Organizations

When we embrace the concept to be of service whenever, wherever, and to whomever is in our lives (including work life), our abilities and natural life energy for accomplishing what we want in our lives is tremendously accelerated. The "garden hose" gets bigger!

What changes do you feel you need to make in order to apply this more in your life?

_____
_____
_____

## THE GARDEN HOSE: KINKING VERSUS FLOWING

▶ **"Kinking the Garden Hose"**
(Desired results harder to get)

1. Don't believe in the Law of the Harvest.

2. Ingratitude.
3. Never say thank you.

Add others that come up for you:
_____
_____
_____

▶ **"Energy Flowing"**
(Desired results come easier, quicker, and more abundantly)

1. Believe in the Law of the Harvest and give forth what I choose to have in my life.

2. Gratitude.
3. Acknowledge people as a normal part of my everyday life.

Add others that come up for you:
_____
_____
_____

What has been of greatest value to you from reading this chapter?
_____
_____
_____

Is there something specific that you want to add to your desired results because of this value?
_____
_____
_____

Is it worth power pausing now to complete a plan for the added result?
___ Yes ___ No

If yes, copy the Change Master Plan form (page 164) and create your future now.

_____
_____

What will be your "I am" freedom statement to support your plan?

**Today, By Choice, I Am...**

_____
_____
_____
_____

CHAPTER ELEVEN: EXPERIENCING ALL

# 12

## REALIZING YOUR FULL POTENTIAL AND FREEDOM

"To give five minutes to the realization of true divine love is greater than to pass a thousand bowls of food to the needy—because in giving forth love, you help every soul in the universe." —GAUTAMA BUDDHA

The one Principle, Attitude, and Practice that encompasses all the others is love. It's rarely spoken of at work and in most organizations of the past. Twentieth century organizations considered the word too soft, and that it has no place in the business world. Love is rarely put in the same sentence as "achieving results." The many "negative" connotations to this word have made it thought unhealthy, risky, and unsafe, especially in the business world.

Love is the ultimate source of total freedom. In its highest form, love is centered in thoughts, feelings, actions, and words that are good and wholesome, so that *the true measure of great leadership is measured by how he or she honor and value themselves and his or her own welfare physically, mentally, emotionally, and spiritually, while doing the same towards all they associate with.*

"Love in organizations...is the most potent source of power we have available." —MARGARET WHEATLEY, *Leadership in the New Science*

"A human being is part of the whole, called by us 'universe,' a part limited in time and space. We tend to experience ourselves, our thoughts, and feelings as something separate from the rest—a kind of optical delusion of consciousness.

"This delusion is kind of a prison for us, restricting us to our personal decisions and to affection for a few persons nearest to us. Our task must be to free ourselves from this prison by widening our circle of compassion

to embrace all living creatures and the whole of nature in its beauty."
—ALBERT EINSTEIN

"Practice. Use anything and everything to get yourself into that active, loving state."   —JOHN ROGER, *Relationships: The Art of Making Life Work*

Most people enjoy popcorn as a favorite movie-watching treat. When you stop and think about it, isn't it amazing that out of each little seed comes something that tastes so good? A little seed pops into a wonderfully big piece of popcorn, almost three to five times its original size. What is it that performs this magic? Heat!

People are like popcorn seeds. Deep and sincere caring—love—is the heat that helps bring out the best in them. With love, three to five times (and more) additional effort is given and energy builds up, and so more power to get results!

In terms of bottom line results, when love is given in appropriate ways it will generate more than what otherwise is experienced. However, like some seeds that don't pop when heat is applied, there are a few who have been so victimized in their past that love will not be received and they are unable to bring out more of their best through caring and supportive efforts.

## Love Versus Fear

Some experts say that there are only two emotions—love and fear—and that all emotions can be classified as one or the other. Your full potential cannot be realized when fear exists. With fear, results are diminished, and they occur with more difficulty and slowly, if at all.

Fear is not all bad, and something that needs to be completely avoided. Emotions of fear will sometimes move us to do things we need to do, things that are in alignment with our values and principles. Fear can be valuable when we choose to use it for positive assistance to achieve.

Fear can help us be more aware of certain situations. It can be a beneficial warning when we are heading in a direction that does not serve our goals.

But fear can also be paralyzing. It is a very strong emotion. It can stop us from taking necessary action in accomplishing things. It is important to find the ways that fear does not stop us, slow us down, or even distract us for a moment.

**147**

CHAPTER TWELVE: REALIZING YOUR FULL POTENTIAL

Definition of Fear:
  **F**alse
  **E**xpectations
  **A**ppearing
  **R**eal

## HOW TO THRIVE ON FEAR AND USE IT TO YOUR BETTERMENT

Avoiding fear doesn't work. Feel it, don't hide from it. Appreciate it and allow it to powerfully propel you forward. Here are some things to help you when fear unexpectedly comes up:
- Breathe slowly and deeply.
- Physically move around, even exercise.
- Get out into nature.
- Sing a positive song you love.
- Stay focused on something positive until the feelings of fear dissipate.
- After allowing yourself to feel it, let go of it and see it fly away forever.
- Know and trust that there is always a gift from this fear on the other side of it. Focus on receiving the gift and understanding what it is.
- Laugh.
- Keep your freedom statements handy and repeat them.
- Go outside for awhile, maybe for a walk.
- Talk to someone about your feelings, or write your feelings in a journal.
- Do something special for your body.
- Talk to yourself positively.
- Get out and serve someone. Do something or say something nice to someone.
- Keep a list of things that you used to be afraid of that you have faced and overcome, then review that list.

To accomplish all that is possible, we need to come from the power of love, for ourselves and for others. With love we can experience miraculous achievements. This is why love is the one Principle, Attitude, and Practice that encompasses all things.

## The Fruits of Deep and Sincere Caring

The world loves a hero. Look at what the professional golfer Tiger Woods has accomplished. People see what he has done as tangible evidence that makes it possible for anyone to consider the impossible. This can be true individually, or for a group of people working together in an organization.

For most of us, we need to see what is possible and then we can more readily do great things. Appendix M, "Sixty Signs You are Increasing Your Power to Love and Honor," shows the possibilities when you have embraced the true meaning of love.

## Personal Leadership in Relationships

In terms of successfully achieving bottom line results, the first priority is to focus on increasing the very best in each individual. The second focused priority for getting more of what we want, is to continually improve our relationships with other people and with our organizations.

This is quite a challenge. One person can achieve great things. When two or more are working together in harmony, alignment, purpose, and commitment, the results are multiplied many times over. Then, one plus one equals more than two! This phenomenon has been described as "synergy."

One-plus-one equals more than two is a truth, and very practical results will occur when this takes place. It just works! Life is all about relationships—first with self, and then with others. There are volumes of books written about how to have effective relationships. Here are some simple, powerful suggestions in three areas:

### 1. Relationships Between People

> "If you want to get the best out of a man, you must look for the best that is in him." —BERNARD HALDANE

See the best in other people. Focus on what they do well and acknowledge them for it. Honor people as valued influences in your life. Remember this powerful law: "Out of little things consistently done and said, come great results."

It doesn't take a lot of complexity to heal and improve relationships. Use the personal leadership guidelines in Chapter Eight. It works. Here is tangible evidence:

A woman came in to a training program that was spread over four half-days. She had a grumpy face, arms folded, disgruntled feelings, and an unwillingness to join with the other 19 or so participants. She made sure that everyone knew she did not want to be there. The trainer's excellent approach to people like this was to honor her for where she was, and not to focus on her or make her wrong, just let her experience whatever she needed to.

On the second half day, the same thing took place. She was stubborn and stuck about how angry she was in having to attend this workshop. Again, the trainer allowed this woman to feel and act the way she did without a lot of attention being given to her condition (also a great practice in any relationship).

On the third half day, she came in with a small grin on her face and with arms unfolded. She even began to participate. Everyone knew something drastic had occurred. The trainer could not resist in asking this woman what had happened. The woman began to get more animated and explained that she had been having some real problems with her team getting along and being productive together. There were some real relationship issues effecting their results.

She did at least listen to the trainer who explained how questions like the Personal Leadership guidelines worked with people and teams. With this training, people are trained in the morning and then go back to work to apply what has been learned and then do the same at home that night. This woman decided to try these questions with her people. She said the results were incredible. Her team had been in the habit of focusing on what was wrong with each other, the team, and the company. They were seeing nothing that was going well.

The Personal Leadership guidelines as applied by this woman immediately turned the focus around and attitudes shifted quickly and their movement towards desired results began to pick up momentum again. She said, "This stuff really works!"

But the story is only half over...

On the fourth and last half day, she came in full of life, excited, animated fully, and participating completely in the training. She took up more time than any other participant with her feedback, questions, and comments. This obvious further shift got everyone's attention even more and the trainer couldn't help but ask again what had happened. She explained that the framework had worked so well that she called her ex-husband (she had recently divorced). They had been up all night discussing their relationship through using some of the questions in the Personal Leadership guidelines, and they had decided to get back together again. The room filled with celebration and excitement.

What is possible when simple, powerful practices are actually taken beyond the learning level to the level of application? This woman is tangible evidence. Months later, the trainer called the company and in the course of the discussions found that the newly reunited couple were still together! It was a powerful example of sustainable results.

Improving relationships is truly an art. There is another very significant concept that is taught by Dr. Stephen R. Covey. He uses the analogy of a bank account. Only he calls it the "emotional bank account" with the relationships in our lives. Simply stated, we need to increase the deposits into this account by being positive, acknowledging the good that is seen and heard with people. If we focus only on the negative with people, then the account gets way overdrawn and our effectiveness is minimal to zero. In fact, children tune parents out! Dr. Covey suggests that we need to maintain at least a ten to one ratio. Ten compliments to one corrective comment (sometimes referred to as judgment/criticism) in order to be truly effective in the relationship.

This concept is very real. It works really well when applied faithfully. What is implied here is that if we want to help someone correct something, we had better pay the price before by having given many sincere compliments and feedback. Then the person is emotionally better equipped to handle positively the so-called negative feedback. But to "barge in" with a relationship and tell things that are wrong or bad with a person just won't work. Great damage is done.

It is important that positive focused observations about people, especially those we have a close relationship with, spoken to them often, are needed for healthy relationships that can handle all kinds of feedback openly and constructively.

What value do these suggestions and the story have for you?

_____
_____
_____

## 2. Relationships of People to Organizations

Remain steadfast in being an example of staying positively focused through the use of the things suggested in this book. Use the Personal Leadership guidelines often, even when it is not "needed" (because of existing "problems").

Use the four C's for sustainable growth from Chapter Ten to assist people and organizations in moving forward with new and existing clarity. Be a leader in influencing as many people as you associate with, and the organization you are part of will eventually take on a renewed culture. Others throughout the company may begin to ask questions about what is going on! The fire of your enthusiasm, support, and positive attitude (yes, these forms of love) will spread quickly, penetrating the negative in producing more results, quicker and easier. How do you think the woman in the previous story feels about an organization that provides this kind of training with these immediate results?

Every organization has its issues and challenges. Be the one who helps and provides personal leadership for generating answers and solutions to those challenges. The challenges you feel being in the organization you are currently part of will likely occur in other organizations you think you should go to because "things in this company aren't good." There are things that life wants to teach and you need to learn. Until you do so and make changes for your good and the good of others, the issues and challenges will keep showing up. If possible, stay put, contribute, learn, and grow ("Grow where you are planted!").

### 3. Relationship of Organizations to People

"What you believe and think about people sets into motion the kind of organization you create."
—PERCY JACKSON, *Manager, Digital Equipment Corporation*

Organizations will enjoy abundant prosperity when they are caring and honoring and flexible with all areas of a person's life. Workaholics are dinosaurs of the past. The separation of personal and work life for people needs the attention and concern of organizations. Organizations are in service to their people, just as the people are being asked to be in service to the organization. Does this mean that organizations will not be successful in the future unless they make these shifts? Absolutely not! But remember, the intent of this book is to get all that is possible in desired results, and more, and get them easier and quicker.

Organizations can better honor their people by adapting the Personal Leadership guidelines for performance evaluations, and doing such reviews more frequently so that continuous feedback and progress can be achieved.

Have the people in the organization you are part of get together in groups, according to the circumstances and conditions of the company. Allow them to make recommendations for the kind of environment they would like to have, then carefully listen to the suggestions. Honor their input and where feasible, respond in actions and changes. This is not a "destination" approach, but a journey that evolves over time.

The organization you are part of should do all that it can, with all the resources possible, to assist people to continually bring more of the best that is within them. This may mean more training dollars for more learning to occur, but more importantly found in the application and practicing of what they already know. An organization may be open to having their people "lead from within." This is risky, and this practice needs boundaries. But allowing this to take place has a great impact on the personal leadership of the people, and on the success of the organization, as people come forth positively with their very best effort each day.

One last thought on relationships: Achieving all that is possible in all areas of life comes from "being" all that we can be in "relationship" to each other. These are the two priorities needing our constant focus in order to achieve the "impossible."

> "Men (women) do not attract that which they want,
> but that which they are."
> —JAMES ALLEN

## Freedom Cycle for Achieving Results

The freedom cycle is a summary of the way life works in its highest form. It is a powerful and proven success formula for abundant achievements. It is like a snowball, rolling down hill picking up momentum and size as it rolls. The only way to prove its worth is to experiment with it and observe what takes place. Through your experiences with this cycle, change and add words that reflect your unique experience, so your own revealed cycle works best for you.

### Love

> "Anyone who is residing in the power of love is never destroyed, never separated, always free, always up, always growing."   —JOHN-ROGER

Love is a deep and sincere caring for yourself and all others, honoring and holding esteem for each person, especially yourself, as a valued person on the planet. Desire the best for yourself and others with all thoughts, communications, and actions. Sincerely believe that everyone has worth, and can contribute to the success of life within relationships and organizations you are part of. Allow people to grow and be their very best, and get better all the time. This kind of love truly brings maximum potential into greater and greater reality.

### Expansion

This relationship with self and others brings openness. A "flow state" allows greater energy (momentum) to take place for accomplishing desired results. It gives people the very best environment to choose to empower themselves in their own lives and the lives of organizations they are part of. Appropriate love brings expansion of the "garden hose" for more energy to achieve more desired accomplishments.

### Truth

This expansion opens you and others to new ideas, answers to your questions, solutions to challenges, and opportunities. It brings creativity to all situations, greater awareness of our own self worth, and the value of others in our lives. It opens up passions that have been partially or totally dormant. It brings healing and allows self esteem to grow and flourish.

### Freedom

Truth brings more freedom into our lives. True freedom brings greater power to get desired results, not just through our hard work, but through who we are. Relationships heal and strengthen. Working together becomes more and more easy. Organizations we are part of gain the ultimate benefits from their greatest assets: the people that make up the organization. Being "on a roll" and keeping the momentum going, is sustainable. Even when challenges occur, they are met with solution-oriented attitudes as we work together in harmony.

### Joy

True freedom creates greater happiness at work, home, and in all aspects of our lives. This does not bring an euphoric bliss where no "problems" exist, but it does bring the power to face difficult situations, conditions, and events with an ability to feel pain, but remain productive and progressive towards greater solutions and achievement.

### Abundance

Joy in accomplishment increases our ability to have a more full and abundant life. Abundance is there for all individuals and organizations to realize a level of success not experienced before and do it more consistently. The freedom to truly achieve our dreams and desires is no longer left to the few. All of us are born to succeed, and succeed more than ever before. It is our right, and our inheritance from "Life." These are not just idle words. They are the truth for those who choose to prove that this cycle works. The results that are delayed for a time, are more than compensated by all the learnings and experience that is gained in the journey. For life, and our unique paths, is not a destination, but a journey of adventure.

This suggested "Freedom Cycle" is linked together like a beautiful chain. Every link is needed to complete the cycle and reap the rewards. Each link is the highest value that is made available to us as human beings living on earth.

Simply stated in summary form: *appropriate love expands our whole being (thoughts, feelings, words, actions), opening us to truth, which generates greater freedom, that leads to more achievements easier and more quickly, that brings joy in our accomplishments, which leads us to even more desired results.*

> "The joy of creating is one of life's greatest gifts. The joy of creating in companionship is a treasured adventure."
> —JENNIFER JOSHUA, *The Joshua Company*

## What Is Really Possible To Achieve As Individuals and Organizations?

If you knew that you, or any organization you are part of, could succeed at whatever you chose to achieve, what great results would you go after?

_____
_____
_____
_____

Power pause for a substantial period of time to evaluate this question. Any initial thoughts?

Infinite potential? Infinite freedom? Infinite results? This sounds great, if maybe a little too "motivational." But it can be true, and so the illustration of an oil lamp on the right is an appropriate symbol of our lives. It is up to you and the people in organizations you are part of. Despite all of the issues and challenges, the new millennium will open us up to what is possible!

### THE GARDEN HOSE: KINKING VERSUS FLOWING

▶ "Kinking the Garden Hose"
(Desired results harder to get)

1. Thinking within limits.
2. "It's impossible."

Add others that come up for you:
_____
_____
_____

▶ "Energy Flowing"
(Desired results come easier, quicker, and more abundantly)

1. Infinite, open, creative mind.
2. "All things are possible."

Add others that come up for you:
_____
_____
_____

What has been of greatest value to you from reading this chapter?
_____
_____
_____

Is there something specific that you want to add to your desired results because of this value?
_____
_____
_____

Is it worth power pausing now to complete a plan for the added result?
___ Yes ___ No

If yes, copy the Change Master Plan form (page 164) and create your future now.
_____
_____
_____

What will be your "I am" freedom statement to support your plan?

**Today, By Choice, I Am...**
_____
_____
_____
_____
_____

CHAPTER TWELVE: REALIZING YOUR FULL POTENTIAL

# Afterword

"As human beings we are like the eagle. The sunlight in that which is unseen is beckoning us to jump. We have no reason, save our faith, to know that rather than crashing down when we jump into something new or into change that has been thrust on us, that we will be given the freedom of the sky. We have the tools. We have the wings. We have the gentle wind. What more are we waiting for? Do we wait to grow old as we stand on our craggy edge thinking that this is all life holds? I say you have grown old enough. It is time to leap into light, knowing only what you know. For in that act of trust, all power is born. And it is not born before you leap; it is not available before you leap. So, I ask you to unfold your silver wings, lead with your heart and jump into the sky. For the sky will catch you and carry you to universes unknown.

"It is the spirit of flight that we are addressing—the freedom to be supported by that which is unseen. As the young eagle takes off from the nest for the first time, he trusts that the air can uplift him, that it can hold him, that it can move him to where he needs to go. He has no reason to believe that the air can do that, save his instincts. He has lived his life with his legs on the nest and upon the rocks. The eagle had no reason to believe he was safe as he jumped. And still, he stepped out into the air and into the sunlight, and lo and behold, he found a freedom and a strength, and a graceful beauty he did not know or had experienced before."

—JONETTE CROWLEY,
*as shared from her friend White Eagle*

There is a hope in the following vision for each one of us, and for the organizations we are part of:
1. Individuals being far more productive in getting the results they seek;

2. Organizations and individuals creating relationships with each other where tremendous success in achieving desired results is being realized;
3. Greater good is being generated, and is sustainable over time, in service to the people being served and influenced.
4. Less effort (quality) is leading to greater and abundant achievements.

We began this book with an illustration found in Chapter One. It showed the difference some of the principles in this book could make in your ability to get what you want in life. If all the things in this book were applied over time, and, more importantly, if you were committed to use this book to stimulate many other things that are important to you and intuitively come as you read and re-read this material, then the illustration has the potential to look like this:

The choice is yours. As this illustration shows, stepping up and probably directing your efforts and standing forth with new dreams and desires for your own life, in service to others and to your organizations, will truly bring greater results.

As we get clearer as to who we are, as we strengthen our integrity and power to live what we know, and as we increase our desires and experience in trusting ourselves and God, we can stand forth boldly, courageously, and uniquely, and say as Mahatma Gandhi said, "My life is my message."

If you are passionate about:
Realizing your full potential;
Are willing to "pay the price" to do that;
Desire to serve others and organizations
   in doing the same;
Want to share your learnings/experiences
   with others;
Call (866) YOU-LEAD!

Thank you for taking your time to read this. Enjoy your journey in the continuous quest of realizing your full potential for all the personal leadership that rests within you, waiting to bloom into full blossom.

## Appendix A: Concepts and Definitions

**The Divine:** There are many different beliefs on this subject; the definition is really yours to determine and name. When referred to in this book, it means that part of us that is connected to something higher than ourselves. Words that are frequently used are God, God within, Spirit, Higher Self, Buddha, and Inner Nature. Use any other words that are appropriate in your life. "Life" is also used to symbolize the Divine.

**ELI:** Enlightened Leadership International, a leadership training and consulting company, whose principles and concepts contributed greatly to this book.

**Energy:** As with the Divine, each person calls "energy" something different depending on their beliefs and experiences in life. Words often used are: spirit, God, chi, life force, and light. In the sports world, "momentum" is used. *Energy is that unseen force that seems to make things happen.* In this book, "energy" is chosen to symbolize that unseen force in our lives that assists us in getting what we need and want in our life, which is infinite in its power and supply available to us. It transcends matter, or physical form.

**Essence:** What is inside of something we see, hear, or touch that makes it what it is. Its fundamental nature, or most important quality.

**Freedom:** The power to get our desired results and more, smoother, easier, and more quickly. A billboard outside of a church reads: "Freedom is the cause of God!"

**Leadership:** The combination of a person's talents, character, communication, thoughts, feelings, and actions that get desired results for the good of their own life, and for the lives of others. Leadership is about experiencing more of the very best within us, in all aspects of our life, and going forth in service to others and our organizations.

**Organization:** Two or more people gathered together for a common purpose. This could be as small in number as a marriage or as big as thousands of people working in a large enterprise. All of the concepts, Principles, Attitudes, and Practices suggested in this book apply to any size or type of organization. When suggestions are directed to an organization, it is assumed to be a "for profit" business. The ideas can also apply to nonprofits and governments, with adjustments to the purpose of the organization.

**Paradigm:** The way an individual interprets, values, comprehends, understands, and perceives their world. It is a creation of the mind. A paradigm is the fixed foundation in our lives that drives our thoughts, words, and actions. Paradigms remain fixed until some experience (internal or external) or new information is brought forth and becomes the catalyst for shifting to a new paradigm.

**Results:** Getting what you want; a word symbol for describing all the things we choose to achieve in life, as individuals and organizations. "Results" represents what some call desires, goals, achievements, intentions, aspirations, and dreams.

**Truth:** Means what is true for you, not the author. However, the highest "truth" that generates the greatest results, does come from many different disciplines of life. Life has been given to each of us as a great teacher, providing us with experiences that accumulate into who we are, who we will become, and how capable we are in service to others.

## Appendix B: Freedom through Personal Leadership

### THE GARDEN HOSE: KINKING VERSUS FLOWING

▶ **"Kinking the Garden Hose"**
(Desired results harder to get)

▶ **"Energy Flowing"**
(Desired results come easier, quicker, and more abundantly)

# Appendix C: Things That Affect the Flow for Desired Results

## THE GARDEN HOSE: KINKING VERSUS FLOWING

**▶ "Kinking the Garden Hose"**
(Desired results harder to get)

Hate.
Unthankful.
Fear.
Egotism.
Resists change.
Negative attitude.
Reactive.
Avoids opposition.
Critical of self/others.
Want to change others.
Blames others.
Feels like a victim.
Anger.
Guilt.
Insecurity.
Thinks excessively in past or future.
Tries to change what is.
Discord.
Doubt.
"I should have."
Complaining.
Feelings of I'm not enough.
Unresolved conflict in relationships.
Heart closed.
Manipulates.

**▶ "Energy Flowing"**
(Desired results come easier, quicker, and more abundantly)

Love; Thankful; Courage; Humility.
Welcomes change as natural process in life.
Positive attitude; Proactive.
Accepts opposition.
Honors self/others.
Accepts others as they are.
Self-responsibility.
Feels in control for directing their life.
Calm; Forgiveness of self and others.
Peaceful and secure.
Stays in present.
Accepting.
Harmony.
Confidence.
Lets go and lets it be.
Observes without judging.
"I am capable of accomplishing."
Harmonious relationships.
Heart open.
Sincere and pure motives.

*Other things that create a "flow state"*
Appreciation of all creation; being awake, conscious; uplifting music; laughter; dancing; reading wholesome literature; play; loving self and others for what they are now.

# Appendix D: Change Master Plan

Date:_____

1. Detailed description of desired result: _____
   _____
   _____
   _____
   _____

2. Why do I choose this result for my life (organization)?_____
   _____
   _____
   _____
   _____

3. Plans:

| Who | What | When | Celebrate |
|-----|------|------|-----------|
| ___ | ____ | ____ | _____ |
| ___ | ____ | ____ | _____ |
| ___ | ____ | ____ | _____ |
| ___ | ____ | ____ | _____ |

4. When emotions try and distract my focus, my plan is:
   _____
   _____
   _____
   _____

5. Today, By Choice, I Am: _____
   _____
   _____
   _____

6. How will I know I am moving towards achieving my desired results?

_____
_____
_____
_____

7. Who will I be accountable to? When and how often will I report back?

_____
_____
_____
_____

Reminders:
    Stay aware—watch for signs of progress and celebrate.
    Diligently focus and persist, no matter what, until you succeed.
    Observe distractions/opposition as they show up and let them go.
    Revise plan as learnings occur through progress.

# Appendix E: How We Are Evolving in the New Millennium

## ECONOMIC, VISION, AND SPIRITUAL PARADIGMS

| **Economic Paradigm** | **Vision Paradigm** | **Spiritual Paradigm** |
|---|---|---|
| (Global Consciousness) | (Vision Consciousness) | (Universal Consciousness) |
| (Most People Today) | (Transition—The Bridge) | (Spirit—Vision—Service) |
| Live from the mind. | Lives from mind/spirit. | Lives from spirit. |
| Fear-based. | Fear/love based. | Divine love based. |
| Doing in order to have. | Doing and being in order to have. | Being/doing/to enjoy infinite having. |
| Competitive. | Collaborative. | Co-creation. |
| Reactive. | Responding. | Being source—totally proactive. |
| Conditional love. | Unconditional love. | Infinite/divine love "I am." |
| Separate—alone/lonely. | Equality—wholeness. | Unity/oneness. |
| Live in the past/future. | Live in the past/future/now. | Lives only in the present. |
| Self-centered service. | Serves self and others/community centered. | In service to God/God-centered for the highest good for all. |
| Blames others. | Sometimes me /sometimes you. | Looks to self as source and looks for the gift within all things. |
| Judgmental/critical. | Discernment/choice/acceptance/forgiveness. | Sees all as divine expression of love. |
| Manipulative/control. | Letting go/surrender. | Intend/allow—prayer and faith. |
| Mission—Goals—Strategies. | Vision—mission—goals. | Consciousness creates. |
| Inauthentic use of power and authority. | Authentic use of power and authority. | Freedom and peace. |
| Lacking trust. | Trust emerging. | Detachment/know the truth from spirit. |
| Competence. | Mastery. | Divinity—our destiny. |
| Wordy and complicated. | Fewer words. | Simple. |
| Having more is being more. | Letting go of all that no longer serves us. | Simplicity and gratitude in all living. |
| Worries/confused. | Centeredness/emerging love. | Infinite joy/lightness. |
| Needs/wants credit. | Shares credit. | Credits grace of God in gratitude. |
| Dysfunctional/wounded/victim. | Healer/healed. | Co-creator with human and divine will. |
| Darkness. | Enlightenment. | Being the light. |
| Effort. | Effort/grace. | Grace. |
| Accountability. | Stewardship—reporting back. | Self-responsibility. |
| Conditional life/takes things personally. | Transformational life/transpersonal life. | Being and living universal truths. |
| Human—man's way | Transitional way. | God's way. "Heaven on earth." |

Created by Barbara Ann Curl, Founder of the Kaua'i Aloha Foundation and the Global Leadership Center of Kaua'i, Hawaii. Used with her permission with some minor revisions by Richard W. James.

## Appendix F: Twelve Habits for Leading from Within (Intuition)

*1. Believe that a Divine source exists and that it has all the answers.*

The highest principle of intuition is to first believe that a Divine source exists. This source has all the answers to your questions and solutions to the challenges in your life. Your faith in the Divine is shown by stopping long enough to look to it for guidance and honor what is received.

The surest way to become proficient at leading from within is practice, practice, and more practice. When the so-called illusion of failure shows up, pick yourself up, look at the learnings gained, and begin again. Do that as many times as it takes until you have gained confidence in this approach to directing your life. Try little things at first, then move up to bigger decisions and needed guidance as confidence through experience is gained. With the highest principle and supportive attitudes, your practicing will make perfect over time.

*2. Slow down...and consistently stop!*

Our fast paced life naturally restricts our ability to look toward and receive guidance from your Divine source. Make the choice and do whatever it takes to slow down your life to look for answers to your questions. You may even stop totally for prayer and/or meditation on a consistent basis.

Practice quieting the mind. Practice thinking about nothing and just resting. Most people find this extremely difficult to do, but it will make it easier to hear and see the answers when they come.

*3. Consistently ask questions that are important to you for successfully guiding your life and the lives of the organizations you are part of.*

At first, questions are doors you open, but as you become proficient at looking inward, the door will fling open permanently and Divine living will flow consistently until it will become a part of you.

Be clear with the questions.

Be specific.

Never ask why out of pain, but to gain understanding and learnings.

The answer you get is in direct proportion to the clarity and quality of the question.

*4. Listen for answers.*

Always look inward. Answers seem simple because they are not clouded by human reason, judgements, perceptions, or justifications. By simply accepting the direction/answers, the "why" will follow naturally.

Stay awake and aware, looking in all areas of life for the answers.

A standard yardstick to measure whether the mind/emotions or the Divine is giving guidance is to observe whether the guidance creates good for you and for others. If not, go back and ask again.

By quieting the mind and stopping the body, the answers come when Life is ready to give them. Trying to force an answer only brings imperfection and uncertainty.

Involve your whole being (body, mind, and the Divine) in this process, for answers come from many seen and unseen sources.

It may be helpful to set aside a certain time of each day that is best for you.

*5. Be willing to learn new things.*

Let go of past learnings that no longer apply in order to let new things be accepted.

The Divine brings newness of life, including new truths that challenge your levels of acceptance, but lead to more goodness in your life and for others.

*6. Courageously act upon direction received.*

Life may test you by being slow to answer, or by not yielding the result you wanted from your immediate action. Persist no matter what obstacles show up.

The sooner you act, the quicker the learnings come (and eventually the actual desired results are created).

Develop trust in the Divine and in yourself.

*7. Be thankful.*

Create a gratitude journal.

Pray.

Acknowledge others who have helped you receive guidance, A great spiritual leader once said: "God does notice us, and He watches over us. But it is normally through another human being that He meets our needs."

*8. Keep a journal and share your successes.*

Write down your questions, the challenges you are facing that need solutions, and record the answers and direction as it comes.

Follow the four C's for sustaining growth in Chapter Ten.

There is great power in verbally sharing successes with someone else.

*9. Freedom statements and affirmations.*

Write down or make an audio recording of your freedom statements and affirmations around the intuition process.

Be committed to read or listen to them often each day.

*10. Service to others, the organizations you are part of, and to all life.*

Reaching out to others with the desire to do good strengthens your power to receive direction from the Divine. This is a law that will enhance your life and intuition.

Donate time and money to charitable organizations. This is also rewarded by the laws of the Divine.

Service is powerful, and you can create great good from even the smallest acts. Greatness often comes not from great feats or acts, but from many small deeds done consistently.

*11. Be a good person.*

The more you seek the Divine in all that you do, the greater the Divine will be available to you.

*12. Develop your intuition with others.*

Working with others helps increase intuition—confidence will build more quickly when others are working at this together.

Sometimes the answers others will get are different than yours, and the information needs to be put all together like a puzzle.

If you are in a group seeking the blessings of collective intuition, have the courage to always speak what is your truth. Don't judge yourself or others when your answer is different from everyone else's. This is not a competition. Just keep focused and practicing and getting more proficient at your ability to draw on this infinite resource while assisting others to do the same.

## Appendix G: Differences in Directing Your Life from the Mind (Logic) versus the Divine

### RECEIVING DIRECTION FROM LOGIC VERSUS THE DIVINE

| ▶ The Mind (Logic) | ▶ The Divine |
|---|---|
| Filters information from perceptions developed in the past. | Lets truth flow. |
| Limitations based on beliefs. | Infinite knowledge/possibilities. |
| Judgements as to good/bad, right/wrong. | Observes. |
| Lives in the past/future. | Lives in the present only. |
| High risk. | No risk—best possible results for all occurs. |
| Justifies and reasons. | Honors feelings inside. |
| Questions. | Accepts. |
| Feels quicker and rushed. | Slow and Smooth. |
| Less loving. | Full of love. |
| Chaotic. | Peaceful. |
| Complicated. | Simple. |
| Operates from "should" and "ought to." | Trusts intuitive directions. |
| Thinking with the mind. | Feeling from the heart and a knowing. |
| Restricting. | Freeing. |
| More uptight. | Relaxed. |
| Lots of activity. | Quiet. |
| Movement in the head. | Movement in the heart. |
| Facts. | Images and feelings. |
| Polluted. | Pure. |
| Motivated by what pleases the world. | Motivated by the simple truth. |
| Seeks acceptance from others. | Seeks truth to serve others. |

# Appendix H: Personal Leadership Questions

## GENERAL LIFE QUESTIONS

### Possible Discovery Questions

- Who am I?
- What are my lesser and greater strengths, and specific talents?
- What is my role and/or purpose in life?
- Who do I want to be? Where am I now in comparison?
- If I had no barriers or limitations in my life as to what I could accomplish, who I would become, and what I would have/own? How can I begin achieving in these areas?
- What great thing would I accomplish in each area of balance, if I knew I could not fail?
- If a genie granted me three changes in my life, what would they be?
- How do I feel about the use of my time?
- What would my ideal personal life be like?
- If I had $10,000,000 what would I do more, better, or differently in my life?

## BUSINESS LIFE QUESTIONS

### Possible Discovery Questions

- What would my ideal professional life look like?
- If I could change anything in my present job/career, what would it be?
- How do I feel about my effectiveness with the people I work with? How can I improve?
- Do I feel technically capable of performing my job? If not, what areas need more strength?

Other business life plan areas to consider:
    Discover your unique gifts.
    Take lessons to improve a talent.
    Take time to work on a hobby, art, poetry, etc.

## EMOTIONAL LIFE QUESTIONS

### Possible Discovery Questions

- What emotional character change would I make, if I knew I could not fail?
- How do I feel about my life?
- Is my self-esteem appropriate to who I want to be?
- Do I feel emotionally healthy? If not, what areas need strengthening?
- Is my life filled with stress? Where is the stress coming from?
- What additional formal or informal education would I like to have?
- Do I plan adequately for my life?
- Do I visualize consistently?

Other emotional life plan areas to consider
    Express your feelings openly and honestly.
    Develop your sensitivity to the feelings of others (empathy).
    Increase your sensitivity to beauty.
    Write your feelings every day.
    Eliminate stress and conflict.
    Make time for thinking and pondering.
    Read stimulating material.
    Build your vocabulary.
    Improve your memory and recall.
    Increase your reading speed and retention.
    Learn new ideas.
    Allow time for doing nothing.
    Read for recreation.
    Make time for solitude.
    Allow time for television.
    Maintain a journal of events.

## EMOTIONAL LIFE PLAN CHECK LIST

| | | |
|---|---|---|
| Adaptable | Flexible | Perceptive |
| Adventurous | Idealistic | Persistent |
| Aesthetic | Impulsive | Pragmatic |
| Alert | Inquisitive | Relaxed |
| Artistic | Intelligent | Self-assured |
| Aware | Knowledgeable | Sensitive |
| Calm | Mature | Sentimental |
| Daring | Methodical | Spontaneous |
| Educated | Motivated | Stable |
| Efficient | Open-minded | Teachable |
| Egotistical | Optimistic | Tenacious |
| Exciting | Orderly | |

## FAMILY LIFE QUESTIONS

### Possible Discovery Questions
- What could I do to improve my relationship with my spouse? (If unmarried, write about the ideal spouse you desire.)
- How could I improve my relationship with my children?
- What specific things would I like to do with my family that I am not currently doing?
- How can I personally improve to increase my effectiveness as a spouse or parent?
- What priority do I give my family in terms of quality and quantity time?
- Do I bring my vocation into my home?
- Does my family feel they can share their feelings openly with me without judgment or fear of criticism?
- Do I frequently ask how I can be a better spouse or parent without being defensive?
- Do I ask each day "What was the best thing in your day?"

Other family life plan areas to consider:
    Meet together as a family every week.
    Plan and set family goals.

Spend time one-on-one.
Listen to and understand children.
Share values and beliefs with children.
Write letters to family members.
Stay close to relatives.
Care for your family's health—dentist and doctor visits.
Vacation with family.
Attend school activities.
Attend extracurricular activities.
Maintain a household.
Shop with and for the family.
Show love to family, physically, emotionally, and verbally.

Spouse possibilities:
Spend daily one-on-one time.
Have a weekly date night.
Plan and set goals for your marriage.
Show affection daily.
Write periodic love notes.
Nurture your spouse's talents and abilities.

## FINANCIAL LIFE QUESTIONS

### Possible Discovery Questions

- How much money would I like to earn? How much money would I like to have?
- What possessions would I like to own that I do not now have?
- Do I feel in control of my finances?
- What would I do if I won the $25 million lottery?
- What would I do the first year (in detail)?
- What kind of life would I live the rest of my life?

Other financial life areas to consider:
Working conditions in your job.
Maintain a savings account.
Work on your career.
Work at a second job to earn extra money.
Spend time with lawyers, accountants, and other advisors.
Read to stay informed in your industry.

Reduce debt service.
Maintain a retirement program.
Pay a tithing and/or making charitable donations.
Select only needed worldly goods.
Care for and maintain worldly goods.
Travel to experience and see the world.
Develop a "mentor/coach" program in your life—someone you are accountable to.

**PHYSICAL LIFE QUESTION**

**Possible Discovery Questions**

- What is my ideal physical appearance?
- What area am I most pleased with in my appearance?
- What physical activities would I like to incorporate into my life?
- What would I like to have more, better, or differently?
- Other physical life areas to consider:
- Eat a nutritious diet.
- Maintain the proper weight.
- Develop self-discipline.
- Exercise and tone your body.
- Get the proper amount of sleep.
- Practice good grooming.
- Get and follow timely medical advice.
- Participate in recreational activities.
- Drink lots of water.
- Read material on good health.
- Read material on the power of human capacity.

### PHYSICAL LIFE PLAN CHECK LIST

| | | |
|---|---|---|
| Athletic | Healthy | Thrifty |
| Attractive | Responsive | Vibrant |
| Coordinated | Striking | Well-proportioned |
| Fit | Strong | |

## SOCIAL LIFE QUESTIONS

### Possible Discovery Questions

- I feel most comfortable in social circumstances when…
- I feel most uncomfortable in social circumstances when…
- Do I project to others what I want in social situations? (greater or lesser strengths)
- How well do I listen to others?
- What is it that keeps me from asking for help or advice?
- Would I like to be different with others? If so, how?

Other social life areas to consider:
  Develop friendships.
  Live the Golden Rule.
  Attend social engagements.
  Get together with friends.
  Join a club or service organization.
  Do volunteer work.
  Be involved in environmental concerns.
  Be involved in civic activities.
  Be involved in political concerns.

### SOCIAL LIFE PLAN CHECK LIST

| | | |
|---|---|---|
| Ambitious | Honest | Reserved |
| Appreciative | Humorous | Romantic |
| Candid | Independent | Serious |
| Cheerful | Loyal | Sophisticated |
| Dignified | Modest | Tactful |
| Generous | Open | Trusting |
| Happy | Outgoing | Understanding |

## SPIRITUAL LIFE QUESTIONS

### Possible Discovery Questions

- What do I feel best within my spiritual life?
- Do I feel a higher power in my life over that of my own abilities? Is it frequent enough? If not, how do I want to improve?
- Have I clarified my values for living?
- Do I maintain a life consistent with my values?

Other spiritual life areas to consider:
- Do silent acts of charity.
- Hold a Sunday planning session.
- Turn to a higher source in prayer or meditation.
- Attend to church obligations.
- Read scripture or other inspiring material.
- Make quiet time.
- Listen to good music.
- Dream.

### SPIRITUAL LIFE PLAN CHECK LIST

| | | |
|---|---|---|
| Believing | Humble | Obedient |
| Charitable | In tune | Prayerful |
| Devout | Inspired | Searching |
| Empathetic | Joyful | Virtuous |
| Faithful | Kind | Visionary |
| Forgiving | | |

## Appendix I: Completing the Past Year and Preparing for the New Year

As you begin looking at any New Year, complete the last year by evaluating and acknowledging what occurred in the previous year. The following questions suggest possibilities that may help and guide you in starting the new year on a powerful and freedom-based path.

- What was your biggest success?
- What was the best decision you made?
- What was the greatest lesson you learned?
- What was the most loving service you performed?
- What was your biggest piece of unfinished business?
- What are you most pleased about completing?
- Who were the three people that had the greatest impact on your life? Have you acknowledged them?
- What was the biggest risk you took?
- What acknowledgment would you liked to have given, but didn't?
- What else do you need to say or do to be complete with the past year?

### CREATING THE NEW YEAR

- What would you like to be your biggest triumph?
- What advice would you like to give yourself?
- What is the major effort you are planning to improve your fiscal fitness?
- What would you be most happy about completing?
- What major indulgence are you willing to experience?
- What would you most like to change about yourself?
- What are you looking forward to learning?
- What risks are you planning?
- What about your work are you most committed to changing and improving?
- What one yet undeveloped talent are you willing to explore?

- What brings you the most joy? How are you going to have more?
- What can you do more of to support your co-workers?
- What can you do to express more love?
- What one word would you like to have as your theme?

## Appendix J: Twelve Areas of Balance

**TWELVE AREAS OF BALANCE**

1. Spiritual . . . . . . . . . . . . . . . . . . . . . My relationship with God.
2. Personal . . . . . . . . . . . . . . . . . . . . . My relationship with myself.
3. Emotional . . . . . . . . . . . . . . . . . . . . My relationship with my feelings.
4. Intellectual . . . . . . . . . . . . . . . . . . . My relationship with my mind.
5. Physical . . . . . . . . . . . . . . . . . . . . . My relationship with my body.
6. Family . . . . . . . . . . . . . . . . . . . . . . My relationship with my family.
7. Spouse . . . . . . . . . . . . . . . . . . . . . . My relationship with my spouse.
8. Social . . . . . . . . . . . . . . . . . . . . . . . My relationship with friends and others.
9. Financial . . . . . . . . . . . . . . . . . . . . My relationship with my career and money.
10. Community . . . . . . . . . . . . . . . . . . My relationship with the world.
11. Possessions . . . . . . . . . . . . . . . . . . My relationship with the things I own.
12. Talents . . . . . . . . . . . . . . . . . . . . . . My relationship with my abilities and gifts.

## Appendix K: Preparing your Personal Life Purpose Plan

**Vision statement:** Core view of yourself.
**Mission statement:** How vision will be realized.
**Strategy:** Plan to implement mission.
**Action plan:** How strategy will be executed.

**Vision Statement**
  Core view of yourself as seen by yourself and significant others.
  Based on values.
  Must be well understood.
  Has to do with an over-arching philosophy
  Does not include many action words.
  Based on a purpose higher than satisfying ego.
  Keeps you motivated.
  Causes you to get going in the morning, every morning.
  It fills you with passion and excitement.

**Mission Statement**
  Creates track to be followed to live the vision.
  Motivates you each day to honor the vision.
  Creates something bigger than yourself.
  Expresses character and competence.
  Takes into consideration past successes and future interests.
  Has to do with goals.
  Includes action words, how the vision will be realized.
  Written to inspire you, not impress others.

**Strategy**
  Describes in detail how mission will be implemented.
  Must be clear, easy to follow.
  Includes "by when" dates.
  Keeps you on track.

How to use resources to execute plan as effectively as possible.
Includes alternatives for unforeseen events.

**Action Plan**
Details how to execute strategy on daily, weekly, monthly, quarterly basis.
Delineates specific plan with "by when" dates.
Includes accountability and check points.
Includes measures of effectiveness for evaluation.

## Appendix L: Vision for Organizations

Vision is the quality that elevates the mundane into the higher realms of achievement. It excites passion, bestows meaning on otherwise routine or dreary days, gives direction to goals and provides guidance to daily decisions.

Vision is a dream or picture of the future which draws us—pulls us—into the future. People throughout the organization can quote the vision statement because they're living it, not because they've memorized it.

### QUALITIES OF A STRONG VISION PROCESS

Vision includes elements that will endure beyond the tenure of anyone currently working in the organization.

Be careful not to confuse vision with the mission statement.

Develop vision completely before attempting to write a mission statement.

Don't substitute strategies, plans, and goals for vision.

All team members give input to the development of the vision.

Vision incorporates (and is) an organizational story, with each point calling specific, vivid, and realistic pictures to the reader's mind.

After thirty days, all team members can passionately articulate the vision in their own words.

Vision statement has at least five major, clear, focused subpoints that commit people to specific paths.

Team members think and feel the vision is worthy.

Vision statement relates to and affects daily decisions by the organization's team members.

Vision is achievable in total and in all its parts.

Customers and suppliers (if applicable) know, understand, and if appropriate agree with the vision.

Vision statement clearly differentiates the organization from competitors in significant ways.

Refuse to borrow any part of the vision from anyone else, or buy it from a consultant.

Vision statement is a declaration of what the organization wants to become, not what is thought others might want the organization to become.

Vision statement has multiple points that neither the organization nor competitors are not doing, but which it is known will have to be done.

Vision has passion to inspire and make the team run.

Vision has aspects about which team members can—and do—brag to friends.

Everyone gives feedback on the vision and mission statement, and feedback is built into revisions as needed.

Believe that the organization can't operate successfully without a vision and a mission statement.

From an organizational perspective, a vision has to have at least five components:

1. A sense of worthiness.

"The greatest use of life is to spend it for something that will outlast it," said William James.

2. An ability to inspire.

"I simply dream dreams and see visions, and then I paint around those dreams and visions," said Raphael.

3. An invitation to share.

"We all need to believe in what we are doing," said Allan D. Gilmour.

4. Clear and understandable detail.

"Write the vision and make it plain upon your tables, that he may run that readeth it," recommended Habakkuk.

5. Achievability.

"I never gave an order that couldn't be obeyed," General Douglas MacArthur answered when asked about his key to success.

A vision tells where the organization is going; strategies tell how to get there; plans and goals tell how to implement and measure strategies. Does a vision tell a story (stories move the heart) about who the organization is, what is believed, and what is valued? When people respond because their hearts and dreams are in tune with the vision, the organization is ahead of 80 percent or more of other organizations.

Ask team members to rate the vision statement point by point, on a 1–5 scale of inspiration and passion.

5. I would do anything possible to help this come to pass.
4. This is very important and worthy of some sacrifice.
3. I am glad we want to do those things, but they don't hit me where I live.
2. I am a little embarrassed about our vision, but I need the paycheck.
1. This ship is in trouble, and I have my eye on the lifeboat.

## Appendix M: Sixty Signs You Are Increasing your Power To Love and Honor

1. I feel happy and calm.
2. I feel truth and new ideas coming up. My mind is clear and I can feel the flow of truth and wisdom flowing naturally to bless my life and others.
3. I feel generous.
4. There is no person on earth that can offend me, take my peace away, awaken my anger, or get me upset.
5. I feel confident in everything I do.
6. I feel very open, willing to have anyone see what I am doing or hear what I am saying.
7. Pain from this life, from any source, feels purposeful and thus a sense of joy.
8. I am filled with hope.
9. I feel outgoing, anxious to be with people.
10. I am glad when others succeed.
11. I am fearless.
12. I bring out the best in others, and say the best of others.
13. I gladly accept community service assignments.
14. I want to be in a place that feels special, even sacred.
15. I feel united with those around me as children of God.
16. I feel like praying to my higher source.
17. I have control over my emotions.
18. I am glad to be alive.
19. I enjoy extraordinary perceptions about life and those around me.
20. I easily discern when someone is not telling the truth.
21. I communicate easily with those around me.
22. I feel vigorous and full of life.
23. I feel playful.
24. I am full of joy.
25. My will to do and be is unusually strong.
26. I can feel great strength of character growing inside of me.

27. I am full of loving feelings for myself, the Divine, others, and all creation.
28. I feel like cleaning up and caring for Mother Earth.
29. I am organized.
30. I am enjoying my unique journey in life.
31. I am attuned to my specific mission here on earth.
32. I have a very powerful sense of who I am.
33. Life generally feels smooth, easy, and perfect.
34. I feel alive and life feels like a continuous celebration.
35. I want to move, speak, and function slowly.
36. I feel very aware of myself, and all things around me that are all connected to a Higher Source.
37. I feel like serving others.
38. I desire to dream and create
39. I feel the power to realize all my dreams and desires.
40. I am in balance physically, emotionally, mentally, and spiritually.
41. I feel the continuous flow of trust in self and others.
42. I feel believing.
43. I feel childlike.
44. I feel best in cleanliness and orderliness.
45. I feel the desire to remove all separateness into a oneness with God.
46. I feel a desire to help others fulfill their dreams.
47. I can see and feel God in all creation.
48. I feel a very high, healthy self-esteem.
49. I feel full of gratitude.
50. I feel humility.
51. I want to continuously learn and grow.
52. I feel in perfect health.
53. I desire to be good, do good, and experience all that is possible.
54. The joy in my heart is reflected through the smile on my face.
55. I feel peaceful.
56. My life is as simplified as possible.
57. I lead a life of integrity.
58. I enjoy making and keeping my commitments.
59. I listen effectively to others.
60. I accept myself and others for who we are now.

These are not absolute. They will get stronger and stronger as time and experience moves forward.

Other signs of the spiritual awakening process:
- Actions based on the now, as it comes, rather than out of fear or what has to get done.
- Ability to enjoy each exquisite moment.
- Losing the natural human tendency to judge others, life, and yourself.
- Total acceptance of what shows up in your life.
- Losing the natural human tendency to analyze others and yourself.
- Seeing more and more how everything fits together. Contented feelings of oneness with others, nature, and self. Treat all creation with the same reverence.
- Losing the desire to participate in or create confrontation, and in making others wrong.
- Trust. No worry.
- Great feelings of appreciation for all of life.
- Feelings of abundance. No feelings of scarcity. Focus on what is, and what you currently have to enjoy.
- What you think about expands.
- You see the world as degrees of strength, light, and warmth.
- Smile all the time.
- Great urges to give and receive love.
- High awareness of the big picture of life. The details of earth life become less important, knowing that all things are coming to pass exactly as it should.
- Always asking, what is this trying to teach me?
- *The greatest sign of true spiritual awakening rests in running on only one real question: What is this experience or person teaching me about love?*

# Appendix N: Freedom Questions

These questions are structured so that people are able to stay open and positive rather than feel defensive or resistant. They facilitate people getting in touch with answers that come from within themselves which creates deeper "buy in" and commitment.

**For your life and your organizations:**
What desired results do you want to achieve?
What would be the benefits of this approach?
What part of your decision are you most comfortable with?
What specifically about that part are you most comfortable with?
What are the benefits for getting past that obstacle? What are the options?
What are you most looking forward to in completing that task?
What does your perfect professional/personal life look like?

**For looking at the past:**
What was particularly effective about the way that worked?
What would you do differently another time?
What have you accomplished that you are most pleased about?
What would be the benefit of doing it differently?
What two or three things about that are you most pleased with?

**For working through issues:**
What have you learned because of this issue?
If there were no obstacles or issues, what would you be doing right now?
In what way could someone be most helpful to you right now?
What other question could someone ask to be helpful?
What has been of greatest value in facing this situation?

**For performance enhancement:**
What characteristics about yourself bring value to your organization?
What areas of your performance are you most pleased with?
What specifically would you most like to be acknowledged for?

How would you describe your ideal self if you were performing at the highest level?

In what ways are you most looking forward to enhancing your performance before your next review?

What two or three improvements have you made in your personal performance that you are most pleased with?

What are you most pleased with as a result of the improvements that you have made?

Who has benefited the most from these improvements?

Of all the things you do on a regular basis, what two or three things contribute most to the success of your job?

In what ways do those things contribute to your success?

What do you appreciate most about your job?

**For selling:**

In what ways is your service/product performing well? What do you especially like about what is provided to your customers?

If you could create the ideal vision of how you would like your service/product to perform, what would it be? How would it work ideally?

If you could accomplish this vision, what would be the benefits to your customers? Your company? Your team? Yourself?

What are the most important areas that must be considered to achieve this vision? What needs to be improved?

**For everyday use:**

What is the best part of your day?

What was special for you about this?

What have you done today for which you would like to acknowledged?

What two or three accomplishments are you most pleased with today?

What is the best thing that happened to you today?

What are you most looking forward to doing tomorrow?

What did you do today to be of service?

How did you feel about doing that for someone?

Of all the things you do together as a family, what do you like best?

Remember a time when you were very happy: What were you doing? What did you like best about that?

What do you like best about yourself?

What did you discover about yourself today that you're most pleased about?

What did you do today to make someone else happy?

What did you learn about getting along with other people today?

Of all the things that happened today, what two or three would you most like to do again?

**For service organizations:**
What does your ideal customer look like?
What are the benefits of this program to your customers?
What are the key benefits of reaching your objectives to your customers? Your company? Your team?

**For projects:**
What have you accomplished so far?
What has worked? What have you learned?
What could you do more of, better, or differently to make sure you and your team are on time and budget?
What support do you need to assure your success?
What do you most look forward to in completing this project?

## Appendix O: Signs of Being a Victim

Choosing to feel like a victim significantly hampers your access to the infinite energy of the Divine. Be aware of the thoughts or emotions of being in a victim condition coming up in your physical body. Here are some signs:

1. Something in your outer world shows up and triggers immediate emotions inside that feel uncontrollable.
2. Blaming something or someone else for what is in your life.
3. Feeling that someone has "done it to you."
4. Feeling out of control.
5. Great intellectual thoughts and emotional feelings say that you need to be right in a given situation, and to do whatever it takes to prove you are right.
6. Feelings of guilt: should have, could have, must, ought to.
7. Feeling "I can't do that."
8. Feeling "If only…"
9. Great dissatisfaction with what is currently in your life.
10. Unusual sense of possessiveness with things or people.
11. Feeling emotionally and intellectually closed down to others.
12. Feeling defensive.

## Appendix P: High Priority Reading List

*As a Man Thinketh,* James Allen
*Breaking the Rules,* Kurt Wright
*Built to Last: Successful Habits of Visionary Companies,* James Collins and Jerry Porras
*Chicken Soup for the Soul at Work,* Jack Canfield, Mark Victor Hansen, Maida Rogerson, Martin Rutte, and Tim Clauss
*Creative Visualization,* Shakti Gawain
*Enlightened Leadership: Getting to the Heart of Change,* Ed Oakley and Doug Krug
*Leadership and the New Science,* Margaret Wheatley
*The Power of Simplicity,* Jack Trout
*Principle-Centered Leadership,* Stephen R. Covey
*The Seven Habits of Highly Effective People,* Stephen R. Covey
*Slowing Down to the Speed of Life,* Richard Carlson and Joseph Bailey
*The 10 Greatest Gifts I Give My Children,* Steven Vannoy

### ADDITIONAL READING LIST

*Creativity in Business,* Michael Ray
*Dare to be Yourself,* Alan Cohen
*The Fifth Discipline,* Peter Senge
*Getting the Love You Want,* Harville Hendrix
*The Greatest Salesman in the World,* Og Mandino
*Healing and the Mind,* Bill Moyers
*Heart at Work,* Jack Canfield
*Influencing with Integrity,* Genie Z. Laborde
*The Inner Game of Golf,* Timothy Gallway
*The Inner Game of Tennis,* Timothy Gallway
*Inner Skiing,* Timothy Gallway
*Journey to Center,* Tom Crum
*The Magic of Believing,* Claude Bristol

*The Magic of Conflict,* Thomas S. Crum
*Manifest Your Destiny,* Dr. Wayne Dyer
*On Becoming a Leader,* Warren Bennis
*Orbiting the Giant Hairball,* Gordon MacKenzie
*Real Magic,* Dr. Wayne Dyer
*The Renewal Factor,* Robert Waterman, Jr.
*The Richest Man in Babylon,* George Clason
*The Road Less Traveled,* M. Scott Peck
*The Roaring 2000s,* Harry S. Dent, Jr.
*Stewardship: Choosing Service Over Self-Interest,* Peter Block
*The Tao of Leadership,* John Heider
*Think and Grow Rich,* Napoleon Hill
*To Him that Believeth,* Frederick W. Babbel
*What Color is Your Parachute?,* Richard Bolles
*What to Say When You Talk to Yourself,* Shad Helmstetter